Railways for Pleasure

Thousands of enthusiasts already derive keen enjoyment from the railways of the United Kingdom; millions more have probably never even thought about it. Geoffrey Body shows how much the latter have been missing in this thought-provoking introduction to Britain's unique railway system. He describes its colourful history and immense variety, and shows that *involvement*, whether as observer, passenger, or even as operator, is the keynote of railway activity as an absorbing hobby. Here is a book that will open up fresh horizons for many, add a new dimension to holiday activity, and certainly take the boredom out of any railway journey.

Widen Your Horizons with this new series
Remember that we cater for all interests. See for yourself with our expanding list of titles.

Places to see

Scottish Islands – Tom Weir
Dartmoor – Crispin Gill

Leisure activities

Good Photography Made Easy – Derek Watkins
Looking at Churches – David Bowen

Sporting

The Art of Good Shooting – J. E. M. Ruffer
Archery for All – Daniel Roberts

Holidays

Canoe Touring – Noel McNaught

Forthcoming titles

Exmoor – Colin Jones
Sea Fishing for Fun – Alan Wrangles
A Guide to Safe Rock Climbing – Patrick Scrivenor
Rowing for Everyone – Christopher Chant

Railways for Pleasure

Geoffrey Body

David & Charles
NEWTON ABBOT   LONDON
NORTH POMFRET (VT)   VANCOUVER

ISBN 0 7153 7213 0

Library of Congress Catalog Card Number 76–8617

© Geoffrey Body 1976

Photoset in 11 on 13 pt Bembo
and printed in Great Britain
by Redwood Burn Limited, Trowbridge and Esher
for David & Charles (Publishers) Limited
Brunel House Newton Abbot Devon

Published in the United States of America
by David & Charles Inc
North Pomfret Vermont 05053 USA

Published in Canada
by Douglas David & Charles Limited
1875 Welch Street North Vancouver BC

Contents

Introduction

Many millions have derived pleasure as well as utility from the railways of the United Kingdom. Very few could describe why railways are capable of giving this pleasure but it has something to do with the colourful history of the system, its immense variety and the many opportunities that exist, now more than ever, to become involved in the skill, excitement and sense of comradeship that a railway activity produces. Perhaps involvement, whether as an observer, a passenger or an operator, is the key word; and the objective of this book is to increase the information available to those interested in railways and thus, hopefully, help them to increase their own pleasure as a result of a deeper sense of involvement.

To obtain the maximum enjoyment necessitates some understanding both of the system and of its origins. In the case of the main line railways these go back to early colliery lines, where horses drew simple wagons over a crude track to the nearest town, port or canal. The first locomotives appeared on such lines, and then on the pioneer Stockton & Darlington Railway which opened in 1825 to become the world's first public railway. The Liverpool & Manchester Railway followed and then the first of the 'main lines'. The 'Railway Mania' was about to produce a spate of building to meet the nation's need for better transport and the investment instincts of an expansionist era. The result was a wealth of proposals, each town wanting a railway and each railway seeing itself as a main line.

Out of this welter of optimism the principal lines gradually emerged, most of them centred on London. The lesser schemes took up their position as feeder or connecting lines and were then slowly absorbed by the major companies until most of the route mileage was in the hands of twenty railways. Each scheme, however small, had needed an Act of Parliament to establish its right to acquire land, and other legislative controls over the worst aspects of competition followed until World War I demonstrated the advantages of less independent activity and more co-operation. The outcome was the Railways Act of 1921 which combined the major railways into four large companies, the 'Big Four'. The Transport Act 1947 completed the process of unification by nationalising all the standard-gauge lines of substance.

Two areas of railway activity were excepted from the 1921 and 1947 legislation. One was the many small independent companies, including the Welsh slate traffic lines. Built under special Acts permitting lower construction standards and simpler operating practices in order to stimulate railways in sparse areas, the lower traffic potential of these varied and picturesque systems made them easy victims for road competition. The other railways unaffected by the two Acts were the many industrial lines, some merely sidings linking a firm with the main line system, others involving many track miles around huge factories or mines, and yet a third group serving tin mines, passing around gravel pits and across peat workings or even sewage farms.

Reproducing the colourful steam railway as a hobby started soon after the first railways themselves and gained momentum in this century as commercial facilities became available. As the steam locomotive disappeared in the face of modernisation and the rationalisation of the railways' Beeching Plan, not only did modelling become more popular but enthusiasts also turned their attention to reviving examples of the real thing. After rescuing the historic Welsh narrow-gauge Talyllyn Railway in 1951, other examples followed until a whole range of private and branch lines had been saved and painstakingly restored to collective private operation. Within and alongside this activity went the rescue and restoration of locomotives, rolling stock, buildings and many smaller items to create a hobby penetrating all aspects of railway activity.

The aim of this book is to place each major aspect of this railway activity in its setting, to explain some of its less obvious features and to describe locations, events, facts and facilities which, hopefully, will increase the reader's enjoyment of this fascinating subject. The book is arranged in three main sections which deal with the preservation movement, the main line railway system and then with the various railway hobbies. The final chapter is devoted to reference information, a short book list is provided and a subject index links the whole work.

If the result gives pleasure it will owe much to many railwaymen and preservation bodies, and especially to British Railways and the Association of Railway Preservation Societies. It will also testify to the considerable help I have had from J. R. Hodson, D. J. Cobbett, Michael Farr, the staff of David & Charles and, not least, from my wife and family.

GEOFFREY BODY

1 The Great Little Trains

'The Great Little Trains of Wales' is a slogan adopted by the preserved narrow-gauge railways of Wales, the area where the great revival of interest in private railways began. Before this, with quaint branch lines and steam traction plentiful, the railway enthusiast had no need to look elsewhere and such private steam lines as did exist were usually of the seaside pleasure line variety or formed part of the hobby of wealthy or devoted men. An example of the latter is the Romney, Hythe & Dymchurch Light Railway which consists of 13¾ miles of 15in-gauge line from Hythe along the edge of Romney Marsh to Dungeness. Still operating with a handsome collection of miniature LNER and Canadian Pacific Railway-type locomotives, this line was opened between 1927 and 1929 by two notable motor racing personalities as part of an attempt both to meet a real public need and to cater for their own interests.

In other parts of the country private lines suffered badly from road competition and the doyen of these, the 2ft 3in-gauge Talyllyn Railway, had been brought to the point of closure by 1950. This 6¾ mile line had been opened in 1865 to serve the slate quarries at Bryn Eglwys but the traffic dwindled to the stage where the company was about to be wound up. The fascinating story of the Talyllyn revival has been told by L. T. C. Rolt in his book *Railway Adventure* which describes how, from a faltering start, supporters flocked to join the preservation society once it had shown that restoration by amateurs could be achieved despite the near-derelict condition of the line when it was taken over. Today over 20 trains operate between Tywyn and Abergynolwyn at the height of the season, many with locomotives and stock from the earliest years of the railway. In fact, so many people have enjoyed the scenery and atmosphere provided by the railway that an extension has now been opened to Nant Gwernol, near the lake from which the line takes its name.

The Festiniog centre

Not far north of Tywyn, the historic Festiniog Railway had lost its passenger services in 1939 and had closed down completely in 1946. Like the Talyllyn Railway, the 1ft 11½in-gauge Festiniog line had been built to

Stalwart centenarian: this tiny 0–4–2 tank locomotive, *Sir Haydn*, just about 100 years old, is still capable of handling this very mixed train on the Talyllyn Railway in North Wales

carry slate traffic, in this case from the quarries at Blaenau Ffestiniog to the tall-masted ships waiting in the harbour at Porthmadog. From opening in 1836 to the introduction of locomotives in 1863 the empty trains were hauled by horses which had then ridden down with the laden wagons as they descended by gravity to the port below. Control of the moribund undertaking was acquired by industrialist and railway enthusiast Alan Pegler in 1954 and, with the support of the Festiniog Railway Society, life was gradually restored to the derelict engine shed and weed covered track. Today veteran locomotives dating back to 1863 and curious double-ended Fairlie locomotives, together with other fascinating items of motive power and stock, operate an intensive service from Porthmadog to Dduallt. Beyond this point the original route has been flooded by a hydro-electric scheme but the society is opening an alternative route to the original terminus at Blaenau Ffestiniog.

North Wales has several other revived lines. Not the least of these is the 2 mile single track of the Fairbourne Railway which started life as a horse tramway. This carried construction materials for the township being built at Fairbourne to meet the increasing appetite of the 1890s for seaside holidays. In 1916 the line was converted from 2ft-gauge to its present 15in by Narrow Gauge Railways Ltd, a company then engaged on constructing and operating pleasure railways. After becoming a victim of World War II the railway was reopened by a group of industrialists and now has an excellent collection of steam and diesel locomotives. These operate a summer service from the main terminus near the BR station at Fairbourne across the sands to Penrhyn Point where there is a ferry service to the neighbouring resort of Barmouth. Still in North Wales are two other lines of note, in addition to the locations mentioned in other chapters and in the itineries at the end of the book. One is the Llanberis Lake Railway which involves a 4-mile round trip from Llanberis to Penllyn. The lakeside route followed is that of the former Padarn Railway, and trains may be worked by Hunslet or Arn-Jung steam locomotives or by one of the company's distinctive diesels. Both this line and the Bala Lake Railway are commercial ventures with a strong sense of dedication to railway enthusiasm. George Barnes' Bala venture consists of 60cm-gauge track following the course of the former Bala & Dolgellau Railway from Llanuwchllyn towards the wild and beautiful Bala Lake, using both steam and diesel traction.

Another Welsh narrow-gauge passenger-carrying railway with its terminus on the coast, thus giving the visitor the benefit of both sea air and scenery, is the Vale of Rheidol Light Railway. The only remaining BR narrow-gauge activity, this exceptionally attractive scenic line was opened in 1902 to serve the beauty spot at Devil's Bridge and the lead mines in the area. It is the same gauge as the Festiniog Railway and came to BR via Cambrian Railways and the GWR, the latter building two of the three 2–6–2 tank engines which now haul the summer trains over the 11¾ miles from the main line station at Aberystwyth up through the wooded valleys, along hillside cuttings, past Rheidol Falls and around a horseshoe curve with suberb views of the gorge below.

Its fellow Cambrian line still operating is the 2ft 6in-gauge Welshpool & Llanfair Light Railway which lies to the north east in the gentler scenery of Welsh border country. This railway was opened in 1903 on the site of a much earlier tramway sponsored by the Earl of Powis and ran from Llanfair Caereinion to the outskirts of Welshpool, where the trains then wound past streets and houses to deposit their passengers and market produce near the main line station. Passenger services ceased in 1931 and freight 25 years later, and although the preservation society reopened part of the line with two of the original 0–6–0T Beyer-Peacock locomotives in 1963, much of their work was destroyed when a heavy storm in the following year swept away the bridge over the River Banwy. With great determination and with the help of the Army the bridge was repaired and services extended to Sylfaen as part of the preservation society's ultimate plan to reach Welshpool again. Interesting features of the W & L line include some foreign locomotives and coaches and items from the former Chattenden & Upnor Railway.

Preserved lines in England

Wales may well be the home of narrow-gauge railways, but there is a wealth of preserved lines in other parts of the United Kingdom. The adjacent West Midlands provides a good example in the Severn Valley Railway, which was closed during the BR rationalisation era but reopened by preservation interests, first over a stretch of 5¼ miles south from Bridgnorth and later over another 9 miles to reach Bewdley. All this was not achieved without considerable legal battles with local councils and some impressive fundraising, but now the railway has not only an attractive route but a very large collection of locomotives, rolling stock and other items. The accent is on former GWR and LMS items but the variety is enormous, with traction ranging from a GWR railcar to 2–10–0 *Gordon*, and stock from a GWR 1902 composite coach to an inspection saloon and breakdown crane.

The northern part of the United Kingdom also has a wealth of enthusiast-sponsored passenger railways as well as John Cameron's Lochty Private Railway from Lochty to Knightsward in Fife and the historic Middleton Railway at Leeds. This was the first preservation project to embrace a freight line, and it is described in a later chapter. Just two years after the reopening of the Middleton line in 1960, the former Midland Railway branch from Keighley to Oxenhope in the heart of Brontë country closed down. By 1968 the 5-mile line had been reopened as the Keighley & Worth Valley Light Railway, and from that time has made spectacular progress. It has built up a collection of some 40 locomotives, a wealth of historic rolling stock and a pattern of services ranging from 30 trains a day at peak summer periods to Santa Claus specials at Christmas. The K & WV locomotives include larger main line examples such as WD 2–8–0 1931 with its now rare Wes-

Ready for its next Bank Holiday service on the Keighley & Worth Valley line: Ivatt Class 2MT 41241, built in 1949. Its companion is a typical industrial 0–6–0 saddle tank of the 1950s: an economical and hard-working design

tinghouse brake equipment and the SR 4–6–2 *City of Wells*. There is another group of smaller main line engines including ex-Taff Vale Railway 0–6–2T 85 and a sufficient variety of industrial steam and diesel locomotives to give a fair impression of the main industrial makers and designs. The rolling stock has a slight LNER bias in its passenger vehicles while the intriguing variety of freight vehicles includes a bogie well wagon, two types of crane, goods brake vans and several ordinary open wagons. The railway has its own musem and the Brontë Parsonage Museum is located in the quaint old village of Haworth.

Another example of how an interest in revived railways can be combined with the delights of the countryside and the fascination of history lies on the opposite side of the county in North Yorkshire. Although the North York Moors Historical Railway Trust's ex-BR standard-gauge branch line was not reopened until 1973, it lies partly on the site of an early horse-worked line which had a 1 in 10 rope haulage incline built by George Stephenson as long ago as 1836. The railway, which again has a varied collection of locomotives and stock, is worked in two sections. From Grosmont to Goathland the trains are steam-hauled, but diesel units normally operate the section to Pickering – partly for better viewing, partly for economy and partly for environmental reasons. This is the part of the line which traverses the lovely North Yorkshire Moors National Park and passes through the Iron Age cutting at Newtondale. Like the other lines the NYMHRT produces its own guide book, which is invaluable in deriving the maximum enjoyment from a visit.

The great little trains of the North West offer quite a different type of attraction. The 15in-gauge Ravenglass & Eskdale Railway has much in common with the Welsh lines in that it started life carrying mineral traffic for the iron works further up the Cumbrian coast. Like the Fairbourne Railway it was revived by Narrow Gauge Railways Ltd in 1915, and changed to carrying both passengers and granite. When the Beckfoot quarry closed in 1953 the railway was offered for sale and was eventually bought by the preservation society.

Today the delightful collection of steam locomotives hauls trains from Ravenglass through woods and along the bracken-clad hillside, finally joining the route of the River Esk for the final stretch to Dalegarth which makes a good starting point for walks up the lakeland valleys. The Lake District has a second preserved railway operating over the 3¼ mile section of the former Lakeside branch of the Furness Railway. The visitor to the Lakeside & Haverthwaite Railway can take a steam train journey behind an erstwhile LMS or industrial locomotive and then alight at Lakeside station to enjoy the prospect of a trip on one of the BR steamers which operate summer services on Lake Windermere.

Sussex—the Bluebell Railway

The South provides some good examples of other aspects of the history and achievements of the preservation activity. The first reaction in the mid-1950s to the economy proposals aimed at rationalising and reducing the main line railway system was the organisation of protests about each proposed closure, and enthusiast preservation only emerged when the energies of protest failed to make an impact on BR. In the case of the Bluebell Railway, which takes its name from the profusion of spring flowers which line its route from Sheffield Park to Horsted Keynes in Sussex, the protestors did delay the original closure and attracted so much attention to their legal battles that sufficient support was raised to reopen the line only two years after BR services were withdrawn. Today steam trains operate regularly, using such interesting steam locomotives as the 0–6–0T 'Terriers' from the former London, Brighton &

South Coast Railway and Metropolitan Railway coaches of the type which might have carried Sherlock Holmes to and from Baker Street. The Bluebell Railway is well worth a visit, not only for its services and over 60 items of stock, but for such curiosities as the period enamel signs on the stations and the delightful Aveling Porter 'traction engine on rails'.

Kent has two lines of particular interest in addition to the Romney, Hythe & Dymchurch Railway. One is the Kent & East Sussex Railway, now reopened after almost 20 years of neglect and 13 years of dogged effort by the preservation society. Originally stretching from Roberts-bridge to Headcorn through Tenterden, which is now the operating centre of the revived activity, this is an historic route in that it was the first to be opened under the Light Railways Act (1896). It is a lasting memorial to Colonel H. F. Stephens who promoted and sustained so many of Britain's original light railways.

Of quite a different type is the 2ft 6in-gauge Sittingbourne & Kemsley Light Railway which started life as an industrial line carrying paper and production materials and was preserved by an interesting example of co-

The Romney, Hythe & Dymchurch services are used by local people as well as by visiting enthusiasts. Here No 3 *Southern Maid* brings its train into Hythe station

operation between an industrial concern and a major railway society, in this case the Locomotive Club of Great Britain. The locomotives have many unusual features such as centre couplings and now haul passenger trains made up of converted wagons. A number of other wagons remain in their original form to represent a further source of interest.

A similar example of preservation lies to the north of London where the Leighton Buzzard Narrow Gauge Railway Society Ltd operates over the southern section of an extensive narrow-gauge sand quarry network. The locomotives of this line demonstrate very well the variety and appeal of narrow-gauge industrial types and they include a vertical boiler example dating from 1877 and two Orenstein & Koppel machines, one a wood-burning locomotive brought home from Africa for restoration. The trains start from a station in Page's Park, Leighton Buzzard.

The two major lines of the South West are the Dart Valley Railway with its headquarters at Buckfastleigh in Devon and the Torbay Steam Railway, whose trains run between a bay of the BR station at Paignton and a riverside terminus at Kingswear. With common operating and supporting bodies, the Dart Valley was the first of the two lines to be opened and now provides a service in the tradition of the former GWR over the $6\frac{3}{4}$ miles of ex-BR branch line to Totnes. Among its many interesting items are the GWR 'Ocean Saloons' which once formed part of trains that ran to Plymouth to provide the first stage of a journey to New York. The Torbay Steam Railway was taken over from BR by the commercial and enthusiast-promoted operating company with the assistance and co-operation of the local authority, a new feature in preservation which is also part of the extension plans of the Bluebell Railway. The original intention to provide full commuter and winter services ran into the same economic problems which BR have encountered in running branch lines; the line now provides an attractive addition to the many facilities of the Torbay resort area, but with services confined to the summer season.

Although these are the longest lines operating the most trains, there are others such as the Lincolnshire Coast Light Railway near Grimsby and the Isle of Man Railway whose services between Port Erin and Castletown represent the last remnant of the quaint steam railways of the Isle of Man, but certainly not the only location of railway interest there. Other locations and items of railway interest are described in later sections of the book and the aim of this chapter has been to give some idea of the origins and attractions of the principal preserved lines that have become a major feature of the British railway scene in recent years. The achievement has been tremendous and deserves support because of its contribution to our industrial history and to the enjoyment of leisure. To facilitate this enjoyment some recommendations about access and equipment appear in the next chapter, and appropriate addresses and 'itineraries' are given in the reference section at the end of the book.

2 Up, Over and Under

A visit to a preserved railway and the discovery or rediscovery of the interest and variety that these lines have to offer is likely to lead to a taste for more. Fortunately there is a plentiful supply of locations, the process of searching them out is not difficult and the hobby has sufficient complications to make it interesting without involving any more expense than any particular individual may want to incur. The task of finding out what activities exist, how to get there, what facilities each location has and what the opening or operating times are is made easy by such publications as the Official Year Book of the Association of Railway Preservation Societies, the Transport Trust's *Historical Transport* and the handy Avon-Anglia booklet *Guide to Light Railways, Steamers & Historic Transport* which also gives timetable information. The main BR timetable gives information on some preserved lines and the local enquiry offices of the National Bus Company subsidiaries will give travel information about bus services in other areas. Comfortable boots and clothes are desirable if the visitor intends to do some exploring when he gets to his destination. Ideally the clothes should be capable of surviving a few travel stains and a weatherproof jacket is useful, especially if it has pockets capable of taking an ordnance survey map, the guide book for the location concerned, a notebook and pencil to record the sights and facts of interest and, perhaps, a bar of chocolate to bolster up flagging energies if a long walk is intended.

All this modest equipment and possibly more might well be needed for a visit to some of the places detailed in this chapter, which sets out to give some idea of the more unusual lines which are not part of the main preservation activity nor offshoots of the main line railway. For example, both a camera and some warmer clothing would be a must for a visit to one of Britain's mountain railways early or late in the season, while an Underground map and a collection of the excellent London Transport brochures make all the difference to the exploration of the LT system. In addition to two mountain railways, the 'up' lines include an appreciable number of inclined or cliff railways, there are pier railways 'over' water and other underground and cave systems in addition to the better known lines of the London Transport area. A municipal tramway remains at work, together with several tramway preservation projects and a horse-worked tram line.

Climb Snowdon by train

Most famous of the mountain railways is the Snowdon Mountain Railway, and this is also the only British example of a 'rack' railway where a cogged wheel beneath the locomotive engages a third, toothed rail in the centre of the track to provide the additional safety and adhesion demanded by the 1 in 5·5 gradient. This 2ft 7½in-gauge independent line was opened in 1896 and rises from its lower terminus at Llanberis to Snowdon Summit where there is a restaurant and shop as well as superb views from the 3,493ft vantage point which overlooks not only the other peaks of the Snowdon range but even such far off points as the Isle of Man.

The locomotives are of special interest and have inclined boilers so that the water remains level over the firebox even when the single coach trains are being propelled on their one hour long journey up the craggy slopes of the mountain. Strict safety precautions operate. Trains do not run in very bad weather, but on clear days the journey is superb and on misty days it has that curious stillness and isolation that reminds the passenger of the other powerful and mysterious face of nature.

The other British mountain railway is similar in length and climbs for just over 4½ miles up a 1 in 12 gradient to the summit of Snaefell in the Isle of Man, 1,900ft above sea level. This 3ft 6in-gauge Snaefell Mountain Railway is actually a form of electric tramway taking current from overhead wires to power its conventional traction bogies. It has the central rail of the Fell system but the horizontal wheels running against this are for braking and stability, not for propulsion. The trains, which run only in the summer, are formed of tramway-type cars which afford passengers an excellent view of the scenery during the 30-minute journey from the lower station at Laxey.

Other inclined railways, albeit shorter ones, are more numerous than might be expected. They are to be found mainly at seaside resorts with steep cliffs and, like the Fairbourne Railway, owe their origin to the nineteenth century fashion for seaside holidays. There are examples at Aberystwyth, Bournemouth, Broadstairs, Douglas, Folkestone, Hastings, Lynton & Lynmouth, Margate, Saltburn-by-the-Sea, Scarborough, Southend and Torquay. Inland, Bridgnorth has an inclined railway linking the lower town with Castle Hill and another line runs in Shipley Glen. Scarborough is notable in having four lines including the earliest British installation which dates back to 1876.

It also demonstrates the variety of this type of railway, which might have single or multiple tracks, vary in gauge from 3ft 8in to 7ft 6in, and range in length from as little as 69ft to as much as 900ft, as well as having differing gradients and a variety of types of prime power. Some lines, like the Clifton Rocks Railway at Bristol sponsored by Sir George Newnes of *Tit Bits* fame, have now disappeared but another of his projects, the one linking the Esplanade at Lynmouth with its twin town of Lynton above, survives and provides a good example of the water-balance method of operation. In this the cars use a common track except at the midway passing point and are linked by hawsers passing around a wheel at the upper station. Here sufficient water is taken into the car waiting to descend to enable it to haul up the other vehicle and provide

Behind Car No 6 on the Great Orme Railway is the Halfway engine house. Note overhead wire for signalling, the central buffer coupling and the double cable running on separate rollers

not only a leg-sparing ride with breathtaking views, but also a very economical form of operation.

The Great Orme Railway, which links the town of Llandudno with the summit of the Great Orme headland, is also worked on the counter-balance principle. Passengers can see the electrically-powered winches which provide additional control from their site at the midway engine house. The 3ft 6in-gauge line operates in two sections. After leaving the terminus in Church Walks, the cars on the first section rise through the back streets of Llandudno until they reach the midway loop, where both the ascending and descending cars push the points over as they leave so that they lie in the right direction for the next journey. After changing to the upper section car, the journey becomes one of gentle green slopes affording excellent views of the town below and of the surrounding countryside and beaches.

The range of 'over' lines is not as great as it once was. No longer can the adventurous ride on the curious Brighton & Rottingdean Seashore Electric Tramroad which Magnus Volk laid along the sands of the Sussex coast and provided with huge elevated vehicles which could continue to operate at high tide. No longer can they join the dockers on the Liverpool Overhead Railway or contemplate a trip on the Bennie monorail system in which a car suspended from an overhead rail was to be driven by a propellor of the aeroplane type. Even the hovertrain appears to have retired from the scene, leaving only a few chair and cabin lifts to represent elevated wheeled transport in the United Kingdom. In addition to 'lines' of this type at Alton Towers, at Blackpool, in the Cairngorms and in the Butlin pleasure camps there is an example at Llandudno which enables the journey up and down the Great Orme to be made using the railway in one direction and the cableway in the other.

Port and pier lines

Railways over water can still be found and these include the train ferry vessels which operate from Parkeston Quay at Harwich carrying a fascinating variety of ferry wagons. Then there is the famous Night Ferry from Victoria, which is such an exciting way to start a journey to the Continent that there is a strong conflict between the interest of the journey and the comforts of the *Wagons Lit* sleeping cars.

Another form of railway which has connections with ships and the sea is the pier railway of which several examples are still at work. Most of these lines were built in the days of regular steamer services when piers had to be long enough to reach beyond the stretches of shallow water to allow the packed excursion and service vessels to call whatever the state of the tide. To save passengers a lengthy walk between ship and shore tramways were provided and several have survived, from the simple 2ft-gauge line along the pier at Walton-on-the-Naze to the once elaborate system at neighbouring Southend. At Southport, Britain's oldest surviving iron pier has a modern 60cm-gauge line but was originally served by a tramway worked by a stationary engine and built in 1863. At Hythe in Hampshire the 2ft-gauge line forms part of a pier and ferry route to Southampton and is used by commuters and shoppers all the year round. In contrast, while services on the 3ft-gauge line on Queen's Pier at Ramsey in the Isle of Man were revived by an enthusiast body, operation is limited to the summer season and is dependent on the availability of volunteers and the renewal of the lease.

The journey from the pierhead at Ryde, Isle of Wight, into Ryde proper was once a separate line and after the new pier was built to extend the train service to meet the steamers, holidaymakers could look across at what had once been a horse tramway. Now the railway system on the holiday island is limited to the coastal route to Shanklin. Where once Adams 0–4–4 tank locomotives (of the type now preserved and operated by the Wight Locomotive Society at its Haven Street steam centre) fussed along with their quaint trains, 3 and 4-car units formerly used on the London Transport system now operate. These and their connecting buses are convenient but they make unromantic travelling compared with the bygone thrill of starting a holiday on the island with an express journey from London to Portsmouth, a paddle steamer trip across the Solent – perhaps with a glimpse of a Cunard liner – and then the slow but colourful train journey which finally reached its climax as the engine burst from Ventnor tunnel and brought its passengers to the sunshine of the resort's delightful climate.

Underground

Prominent among the railways 'under' the ground is the system of London Transport. Controlled from the headquarters at 55 Broadway, Westminster, London SW1H 0BD the system comprises the Metropolitan, Central, District, Northern, Picccadilly, Bakerloo, Victoria and Circle lines totalling 252 route miles, excluding the effect of the Heath-

Beyer Peacock 4–4–0T of 1886, built to work London Metropolitan Railway trains before electrification, and now in the London Transport Museum at Syon Park. Note open cab and condenser pipe from cylinder to water tank

row Airport extension, the embryo Fleet Line and the transfer of the Northern Line's Highbury branch to BR as part of the Kings Cross electrification scheme. The network originated with the 1863 sub-surface section of the Metropolitan Railway between Paddington and Farringdon Street, the first bored tube railway to survive being the City & South London Railway opened in 1890. In addition to the workaday routes there are several lines of special interest including the peak hour Aldwych branch and the line to the exhibition hall at Kensington (Olympia). Contrasts are provided by the modern, semi-automatic Victoria Line and the Epping to Ongar section of the Central Line. This was originally part of a Great Eastern Railway suburban branch line from Stratford, continued with steam trains even after tube trains took over the route to Epping and is still a self-contained service revealing its origins in its platforms and station buildings. Links with the main line system appear strongly at other places. At Farringdon the former GN goods depot stood adjacent to the junction for the line to Bricklayers Arms; at Liverpool Street the connection with the East London section can still be seen; and at Bank passengers can get to Waterloo by using the five-car SR green trains of the Waterloo & City line.

The London Transport underground system has come a long way from the days of 'Twopenny Tube' and the locomotive hauled trains of the Metropolitan Railway. It is hard now to imagine the original steam locomotives condensing their own steam and drawing trains in which invitations to enjoy the pleasure of living at Pinner or Harrow surmounted the plush seats in each staid compartment. Even so a journey on the 'Met' is still very worthwhile. To pass a Bakerloo train at speed is a reminder of the differing tunnel gauges; the activity at Neasden gives some idea of what lies behind the scenes in keeping this intensive system at work; and the modern signalling, with all the refinements of joint automatic and manual control and with some posts bearing 'fog repeaters' to depict the situation ahead in bad weather, provides a clue to some of London Transport's latest developments which include computerised control with programmed timetable information actuating signals and points.

London Transport has always been very publicity conscious and some of the posters of former times have become collectors' items. Good reproductions are available from the Publicity Poster Shop at St James's

What you see from the miners' tramway, used to take visitors through the reconstructed galleries of Llechwedd Slate Caverns, Blaenau Ffestiniog, North Wales

Park Station and there is an excellent series of booklets dealing with the history of individual lines. Other London Transport publications, such as *Visitor's London*, contain useful information about the system and the places of interest to which it gives access and a whole range of leaflets and brochures deal with such special subjects as 'London's river'.

Less well known is the 6½ mile underground system serving 15 stations in Glasgow. Operated at 600 volts, the 4ft-gauge system dates from 1897 and was converted from cable haulage to electric operation in 1935. Another 'underground' line conveys passengers into a reconstructed slate mine at Llechwedd Slate Caverns, Blaenau Ffestiniog. Here a most imaginative scheme has reopened some of the tunnels of the old mine and uses a 60cm-gauge miners' tramway to enable visitors to see the old workings and the exhibits that have been mounted in them. Many more underground lines exist in the industrial setting of coal and iron ore mines and in tin, china clay and similar workings but these are not normally open to the public except as part of a visit by a responsible society.

The underground tunnels and overhead wires of the once numerous tramway systems have now largely disappeared, but a few tramway locations remain. Municipal undertakings are represented by Blackpool where modern tramcars operate over the 11 miles from the South Shore to Fleetwood Ferry and the very different system at Douglas, Isle of Man. Here the summer visitor can join a horse-drawn tram at Victoria Pier, change at Derby Castle to the tram trains of the Manx Electric Railway and then alight at Laxey to round off the trip by riding to the summit of the Snaefell Mountain Railway. A 2ft 9in-gauge tramway operates in summer from a riverside terminus at Seaton in Devon and working tracks have been included in the extensive preservation activities of the Tramway Museum at Crich, Derbyshire. Both here and at the museum location at Carlton Colville near Lowestoft typical street surroundings are being created for the restored trams, further examples of which are to be found at Syon Park, Brentford, at the Glasgow Museum of Transport and in other municipal and enthusiast collections.

3 Business and Pleasure

The railway preservation movement in Great Britain has achieved more than just finding a way of catering for its own enjoyment. Because of the very real considerations of cost and safety which arise when operating a public service the preservation bodies have learned to manage their affairs in a business-like way and this has helped to make them more imaginative and their services more varied. In addition there are other railway systems which operate solely as a business, some which represent a business part of the leisure industry and yet others which exist more to give satisfaction than to make a profit. This mixture has added considerably to the total number of operating lines.

One remaining private freight railway still at work is the Derwent Valley Railway, which once ran from Layerthorpe Station at York to Cliff Common on the North Eastern Railway's Selby to Market Weighton line. Passenger services ceased in 1926 and the standard-gauge track now runs only as far as Dunnington. Despite this, daily freight trains still serve a significant number of industries, including a coal concentration depot at Layerthorpe, and exchange a considerable volume of traffic via the BR connection there. Also in Yorkshire is the historic Middleton Railway, the major preservation scheme founded on freight traffic. The route between Tunstall Road and Middleton Woods at Leeds is close to the alignment of a 4ft 1in-gauge coal tramway authorised as long ago as 1758. The locomotives of the Middleton Railway include some industrial types of special interest as well as the 1895 Danish State Railways engine 385. They still transfer some private siding traffic to and from British Railways as well as providing weekend visitors' trains.

Other lines with strong freight associations include the Foxfield Light Railway, where the preservation society operates visitors' trains over a former National Coal Board line placed in their custody by the present owners, Tean Minerals Ltd. As on the Middleton Railway, former industrial locomotives and rolling stock are used and the trains are allowed half an hour for the 4 miles through attractive Staffordshire countryside from Foxfield to Blythe Bridge. Operation is on Sunday afternoons from April to September. Further south, at Liphook in Hampshire, Hollycombe House has a railway and fairground complex in which one of the lines uses an Aveling Porter standard-gauge version of a road steam locomotive, and the other runs to a former quarry which is now a vantage point for viewing the South Downs. A short freight line is also associated with the Herefordshire Waterworks Museum project at Broomy Hill, Hereford, and with the Brockham Museum Trust's narrow gauge railway museum project, currently moving from an old quarry near Dorking. Altogether there are more than 60 items in the Brockham collection, including ex-Penrhyn Railway quarrymen's coaches and a Maen Offeren incline man-rider car.

Miniature lines

In contrast to these examples of freight working lines and equipment the United Kingdom has a great many miniature railways devoted to providing pleasure rides. Most are to be found at seaside resorts and in parks and gardens, especially zoological gardens. Most have at least one feature of special interest too and many are small miracles of miniature engineering and operation. Several stately homes have very good miniature railways and these include the 1 mile woodland route which crosses back and forth across the River Cam in the grounds of Audley End House in Essex. Similar in length is the Rio Grande-style line in the 160 acre entertainment park at Drayton Manor near Tamworth and the A-shaped layout in the Pleasure Beach complex at Blackpool. The Great Cockrow Railway, Lyne, Surrey is a good example of a fully-signalled miniature railway while the line at Stapleford Park near Melton Mowbray not only has steam and diesel locomotives and a tunnel as well, but trains connect with miniature liners on the lake. Miniature trains and boating can also be combined at Brooklands Boating Lake & Pleasure Park at East Worthing.

Animals and railways have been found together more than ever since David Shepherd brought the East Somerset Railway at Cranmore into being with some of the proceeds of his paintings, and then developed the activity to further the cause of the wildlife he so often paints. Another recent example, of what at first sight would seem an unlikely pairing, is the Whipsnade & Umfolozi Railway which runs through animal paddocks at Whipsnade Zoo and uses old steam locomotives from the former Bowater's line at Sittingbourne. The lions at Longleat had earlier

Typical of a number of interesting pleasure centres, Bicton Gardens operates steam and diesel locomotives on its Bicton Woodland Railway

learned to vie with the 15in-gauge steam, diesel and electric railcar line in the grounds and the combination of animals and railways also appears at Chessington, Dudley and Paignton Zoos. There is a nature reserve near the Lord O'Neill's railway at Shane's Castle, Antrim, Northern Ireland, although the 3ft-gauge of this line puts it outside the normal range of 5in to 24in gauges found on miniature lines. There is a zoo and a miniature railway at Wicksteed Park, Kettering, while at Dodington Park near Chipping Sodbury the choice embraces not only the miniature railway but carriage rides behind handsome trotting horses, a carriage museum, the charming Codrington house and an adventure playground for the children. In complete contrast are the two Scottish lines used to convey guests to and from the grouse moors.

Many other smaller lines may defy grouping into distinct classifications but this in no way diminishes their interest. A good example is provided by the Bicton Woodland Railway. Located at Bicton Gardens near Budleigh Salterton, this 1ft 6in-gauge line was established with locomotives and equipment formerly in use at Woolwich Arsenal. The gardening enthusiast can also enjoy the magnificent gardens laid down in 1735 by André le Nôtre and then take some refreshment or visit the shop before riding on the period shooting brake to the countryside museum, where the very ably presented collection includes a full size agricultural steam engine as well as many smaller tools and utensils of yesteryear. Plants also form part of another varied location, this time near Diss in Norfolk. Here Alan Bloom started adding railway and other steam items to his horticultural nurseries until the former became almost as big an activity as the latter, and the regular weekly open days brought crowds of enthusiasts to savour a footplate ride or the carefree nostalgia of the fairground gallopers. Excluding the short length of standard-gauge track there are three railways at the Bressingham Steam Museum, as the collection is now called. One is a 9½in-gauge miniature railway, another is the 15in-gauge Waveney Valley line worked by two 4–6–2 Krupp locomotives and the third, the 1ft 11½in-gauge Nursery Railway, uses a variety of industrial motive power. Altogether the various lines total 5 miles.

In the West Midlands, at Chasewater Park, Brownhills, Staffordshire, the Railway Preservation Society operates the 2 mile Chasewater Light Railway on certain summer Sundays. The society successfully undertook so much rescue and restoration work that it outgrew its original depot at Wednesford and moved on to the present location, where the operation will eventually be a major attraction of the Chasewater Pleasure Park scheme. Not only has the RPS gathered together one of the finest collections of small relics in the country; it also has some interesting motive power and rolling stock items. The latter, just to quote a few examples, include a Great Eastern Railway 6-wheel coach, a Midland Railway royal saloon and an 1890 weedkilling vehicle.

Cornwall is as much a county of contrasts when it comes to railways as it is in its scenery and in its industries. Standard-gauge lines serve both the holiday traffic and the extensive china clay activity while a new venture, the Lappa Valley Railway, represents a pleasure line operating in a traditional mining area. The 15in-gauge steam trains follow the route of the former Newquay to Chacewater branch line, starting from Benny Halt and conveying passengers to East Wheal Rose where there is an old mine, a cafe and a lake. Further to the south the 7½in-gauge Forest Railway at Dobwalls, Liskeard has a very severely-graded route for a miniature railway and includes several embankments, cuttings and tunnels on the fully signalled 1 mile journey.

Daniel Lloyd's 7¼in-gauge Hilton Valley Railway at Hilton House near Bridgnorth makes yet another location of railway interest in this area. It is also a worthy cause both in earning money for charity and in providing a good example of operation with colour light signalling and electric points. Five of the nine locomotives are steam, and at some of the summer Sunday afternoon and Bank Holiday openings these can be seen working in pairs, 'double headed' to handle the heavy trains. Another private venture helping a good cause, this time church restoration, is the Reverend Teddy Boston's Cadeby Light Railway at Cadeby Rectory, Nuneaton. On one Saturday in each month the line is open to the public and in addition to travelling on the short, 2ft-gauge run visitors can enjoy the small steam museum and marvel at the 4mm scale model railway layout with its 50 locomotives. Many more small private railways are operated by individuals and groups all over the country. Among those allowing some degree of public access are the North Eastern Railway at Haswell Lodge, County Durham where four locomotives operate a 15in-gauge line to the practices of the former NER main line system, the tiny 3½in-gauge Barton House Railway at Wroxham, Norfolk with its Midland & Great Northern Joint Line signal equipment, and the West Lancashire Light Railway at Hesketh Bank near Preston.

One other group of railways which has a great deal to offer both in terms of viewing and of participating is the various preservation schemes which have either just come to fruition, are still hoping to operate public services or which work trains just for members and day members only. Some of these schemes are described in more detail in the following chapters but two of those already running trains regularly provide interesting examples of the differing ways in which this type of activity has developed. In some ways the struggle of the North Norfolk Railway reflects the early history of the line its enthusiast operators have restored. The largely rural M&GN Joint Railway was an obvious candidate for closure by BR and when the preservation body took over the stretch from Sheringham to Weybourne it had no major population centres from which to draw support and no special help in the way of patronage or local authority backing – very much the situation which must have existed throughout the line's history. Starting with two GER locomotives, the activity has been slowly built up until it comprises the headquarters at Sheringham station and a small relics museum there, a varied collection of locomotives and rolling stock and the 2¾ mile section of track, which not only carries regular steam services but may also be extended if the latest plans of the dedicated supporters are realised.

The Main Line Steam Trust, again like the stretch of former Great Central Railway between Loughborough and Belgrave & Birstall that it is reviving, appeared much later on the preservation scene. Despite this and the heavy financial burden of restoring a real main line service, this body has made rapid progress on its headquarters and new locomotive shed at Loughborough Central station and has started running weekend train services under BR supervision. Another ambitious project is the West Somerset Railway's scheme to restore services to the Taunton to Minehead line, one more indication that the impetus of railway preservation is no more likely to be daunted by economic stringency than it has been by the many other obstacles it has encountered and overcome.

4 Preservation in Practice

Railway preservation is not new, of course, nor is it confined to operating lines. The municipal museums have been restoring and displaying items for many years although their efforts have often been restricted both by the lack of money and space and by the claims of other and older branches of history. Notable among the exceptions has been the Science Museum in South Kensington which displays ten representative locomotives and has a very good collection of models. The models at Derby Museum are also well worth seeing and, by a curious coincidence, both these establishments have recently expanded into wider fields. The Department of Education and Science operates the new National Railway Museum at York where it has gathered together the best of the locomotives and other items from the former York Railway Museum and the disbanded British Transport Museum at Clapham. In contrast to this excellent conventional presentation is a scheme in which the Derby Museum, the local authorities and a collection of enthusiasts are cooperating on the Midland Railway Project which will portray the main features of this company in a complex which embraces a working line, a station, workshops, carriage sidings and many other items. Already over 50 locomotives, coaches and wagons have been acquired.

Other local authorities are also developing or supporting such schemes for presenting restored railway items in their natural outdoor setting. At Beamish Hall, 6 miles south west of Newcastle, the North of England Open Air Museum is recreating the industrial history of the area on two sites which not only have examples of locomotives and rolling stock but also enable the visitor to ride in a period tramcar to visit the colliery area or see a horse gin which has been rebuilt on the farm site. In Leicester the Museum of Technology, newly reconstituted, has taken over items from the former Leicester Railway Museum and is creating a new museum devoted to East Midlands industry where the locomotives will appear with exhibits as diverse as bicycles, a fire engine and an aeroplane. The whole site is being developed around the four huge pumping engines of the Abbey Pumping Station in Corporation Road, Leicester. In Shropshire the Ironbridge Gorge Museum Trust has included railways in its very comprehensive scheme for displaying the industrial history of the area. The Trust's Blists Hill Industrial Museum, not far from its other location at Coalbrookdale, includes not only a typical period goods terminal but also a foundry, a mine, a stretch of canal, pumping engines and the notable Hay incline. Enterprise on the site includes not only the usual opportunity to purchase publications and refreshments but also a potter at work and a period printing press.

Among the other main municipal or local authority enterprises are the Glasgow Museum of Transport which has a number of locomotives and trams, the Ulster Folk & Transport Museum in Belfast with its 12 locomotives the Birmingham Museum of Sciences and Industry with four locomotives and the Staffordshire County Council Industrial Museum at Shugborough Hall, Great Haywood. The Borough of Thamesdown has a museum devoted entirely to the GWR at Faringdon Road, Swindon. The vast area of the town devoted to the railway locomotive and engineering works is shrinking, but an imaginative scheme which has modernised and preserved a group of old railway houses instead of demolishing them demonstrates the regard the town of Swindon has for its railway history. The museum itself not only includes full size loco-

Superbly restored by the Scottish Railway Preservation Society: an 1876 Neilson locomotive, *Kelton Fell*, seen here with two wagons. Many preservation societies pay as much attention to freight locomotives and stock as to passenger activities

motives but also signals, nameplates and many smaller items. A room is devoted to Brunel while other exhibits and displays embrace signs, notices, timetables, railway cutlery and china, uniform caps and buttons, company seals and other pieces of railway paraphernalia, each of which not only repays study for its own sake but also adds to the visitor's understanding of the colourful jigsaw of railway history.

Splendid work by amateurs

While these major museums have certain advantages in terms of their professional and presentation skills, the amateur and semi-amateur preservation bodies have made important contributions in making the enjoyment of the past part of an outdoor working activity, in amassing dedicated collections and in presenting the results of their efforts in the informal atmosphere of an open day or a converted railway building.

A good example is the Quainton Railway Society which not only displays main line, industrial and London Transport locomotives at its Quainton station site near Aylesbury, but also operates a short stretch of line there. A length of 2ft-gauge track also forms part of the attractions of an open day at the Dowty Railway Preservation Society's site at Ashchurch in Gloucestershire. Further north, the Southport Locomotive & Transport Museum Society has created its Steamport enterprise in the former locomotive shed at Derby Road and, in addition to its exhibits associated with the former Lancashire & Yorkshire Railway, will operate a short length of standard-gauge line. Nearby, the East Lancashire Railway Preservation Society has taken over the Castlecroft Road Goods Shed at Bury as the headquarters for its locomotive collection and line restoration plans.

While the railway enthusiast is unlikely to tire of the attractions of these locations and their essentially varied collections, it is possible to study individual aspects of railways in greater depth at such locations as the Monkwearmouth Station Museum in Sunderland. This classical station building of 1848 has been restored and now permits the visitor to see a booking office through the eyes of the man who once flicked the tickets from the wooden racks, dated them in the sturdy dating machine and collected the travellers' money with sufficient accuracy for it to match the book total required by comparing the consecutive number of each ticket series at the end of a shift with the numbers which had appeared in the books at the end of the previous turn of duty.

In a totally different context the narrow-gauge museums of Wales add much to the understanding and enjoyment of the history of narrow-gauge railways and complement the activities of the operational lines. An example is the Narrow Gauge Railway Museum at Towyn which has locomotives of eight different gauges, while the National Trust collection at Penrhyn Castle near Bangor includes such unusual exhibits as the velocipede *Arthur* from the former Padarn Railway. Visitors to the castle can also compare a quarryman's coach from the Penrhyn Railway with Lord Penrhyn's own saloon as well as enjoying the historic building and its attractive grounds. A small exhibits museum has been established near Machynlleth by devotees of the Corris Railway who are as interested in their, albeit smaller, piece of railway history as are the many members of the Great Western Society with its depots at Didcot, Bodmin and Taunton. Only the first two of these are open to the public but at Didcot, which is the larger of the two, members of the society have brought 'God's Wonderful Railway' back to life again in the very appropriate setting of a former engine shed.

World of the locomotive

The locomotive has been the heart of the railway ever since the earliest days when the visionary saw it as heralding a new era of prosperity and the gloomy prophesied that it would cause pregnant women to miscarry and all manner of other ills. It is not surprising that these highly varied and infinitely exciting machines should have their own special place in the preservation scene with several locations devoted entirely to them. The Steamtown Railway Museum is a good example with its setting in the former LMS engine shed at Carnforth and a collection of over twenty main line and industrial locomotives, including French, German and Danish types. In quite a different vein is the Birmingham Railway Museum at Tyseley, Birmingham. Again it is the home of a number of locomotives but the setting is an engineering one. In the tools and equipment the visitor can see something of the skills of the locomotive engineer and begin to understand how he tackled a cracked mainframe or a broken piston rod.

At the Dinting Railway Centre at Glossop a special exhibition hall has been built to house and display the locomotives cared for by the Bahamas Locomotive Society as part of its operational steam centre concept. David Shepherd has added to the preservation work in this sphere with

The Barclay well tank locomotive on the Shane's Castle Railway, Antrim, Northern Ireland – a beautiful wooded run along the edge of Lough Neagh which helps preserve the traditional Irish light railway gauge of 3ft

37

his reconstruction of a Victorian era engine shed at Cranmore. Sharing of locations is a common practice in the preservation world, occurring for instance at Hereford, where the 6000 Locomotive Association acts as stewards to GWR 4–6–0 6000 *King George V* at the Bulmer Railway Centre where the cider-making firm house their other locomotives and those of the Worcester Locomotive Society.

Preserving the lines

One other major area of preservation activity is that of the line preservation bodies which are collecting items for use on the railways they intend to open or reopen. Major schemes include the proposal to reopen at least part of the Welsh Highland Railway where one day the station building activity at Porthmadog may be the start of a journey over this superb Snowdon route by way of the Afon Glaslyn, the plan of the Peterborough Railway Society to extend its activities at the Wansford Steam Centre to running a line through the proposed Nene Park, and two schemes in Scotland. The latter cover the plan of the Strathspey Railway Association to reopen between Boat of Garten and Aviemore, and the Scottish Railway Preservation Society's intention to add to its long standing museum activity at Falkirk an operating line between Alloa and Dollar. Other schemes include those of the Swanage Railway Company, the Winchester & Alton Railway and of the South Tynedale, Teifi Valley, Flint & Deeside, Cambrian Railways and North Staffordshire societies. Many of these ventures have interesting supplementary connections like that of the Shackerstone Railway Society which is linked with the Ashly Canal Association and the Yorkshire Dales Railway which holds rallies at its Embsay Vintage Transport & Steam Centre.

In addition to the opportunities they provide to join in the preservation movement by working as well as just looking, the line preservation bodies provide an opportunity through their open days to see railway work from behind the scenes. A visit to the Dean Forest society's activity at Parkend, the Stour Valley's scheme at Chappel & Wakes Colne in Essex or the Bristol Suburban Railway Society location at Bitton may well reveal a locomotive without its cladding, a compartment interior stripped to its main frame and steam heating apparatus or a signal lever frame with work taking place on the counterweights or signal rod connections.

For years people have been forecasting an end to the rapid and continuing increase in the enthusiasm for railways, but one of the reasons why this has not happened may well be this sheer variety that can be found in the preservation scene. Whether it be the stylish presentation of the London Transport collection items in Syon Park, Brentford or the informal mixture of railways, cars and aircraft at the Lytham Motive Power Museum, the variety is still very evident. On an area basis the devotee might join the Plymouth Railway Circle and work on the restoration of the two 4ft 6in 'Dartmoor' gauge Lee Moor tramway engines, and in his spare time admire the last surviving broad-gauge locomotive on its plinth at Newton Abbot station or visit the Port of Par to see steam still at work. Even working involvement is just as varied with the tasks on operating lines ranging from 'lighting up' the locomotive to keeping the hedges trimmed, and if something even more personal is required a visit to one of the smaller museums, such as the Somerset Railway Museum or the Winchcombe Railway Museum, will show that a display of one's own is by no means impossible.

Preservation in Practice

Restoring and operating a railway sounds like a healthy, colourful pastime with plenty of open air fun and the opportunity to discuss the activities with kindred spirits afterwards. It is, of course, all these things and more, but there are complications which require special understanding and effort if the project is to succeed. Fortunately understanding these complications and dealing with them, although making the work harder, also increases the satisfactions. This section is designed to explain what is involved in the preservation movement, to indicate what skills the operating lines and other major activities call for and how they are put to use. In the process it may give the reader some help in deciding where his contribution will be most worthwhile and give him the greatest sense of pleasure and achievement.

For those who want to be involved in a scheme for operating a railway there is still a great deal of opportunity, as the preceding chapters will have shown. They will be the successors to the commercial enterprise of Narrow Gauge Railways Ltd in the years around World War 1 and to the pioneering spirit that revived the Talyllyn Railway and started the great upsurge of preservation of the present era. This scheme may not have had any previous experience to draw upon or anything like the

The preservers at work – a typical scene with a locomotive in steam and sales stands to raise funds for the Parkend–Lydney line restoration. Note the differing sizes of the upper quadrant signals

public awareness that exists today, but it did have several advantages that later schemes did not enjoy. These included the existence of an owning company well disposed towards the idea – at least one later scheme foundered because the shareholders in a moribund company could not be traced – and a narrow-gauge line which had not been out of use for a long time and did not run through any areas coveted by commercial developers or road planners.

The other major change since the historic reopening of the Talyllyn Railway is the cost of preservation. Enthusiasm may well be the first requirement for success but financial resources come a close second. No longer can a group of enthusiasts reduce their initial costs by buying up the assets of a moribund company. Particularly where a BR line is concerned, the process of acquiring ownership is long and costly. The usual procedure is to start by leasing a base by negotiating with the BR surveyor's department, to extend this to the lease of a line and eventually to purchase both. The representatives of British Railways will be helpful if they can be convinced that the project has a chance of success, but their approach has to be a commercial one and recognise not only the value of the land and buildings they are handling but also the work they and other railway departments may be called upon to do to help the project to succeed.

Raising the money

The capital requirements of a preservation scheme vary from project to project. When the North Norfolk Railway floated its company it set a target of £30,000 but the recent plans to acquire the stations and trackbed of the Winchester to Alton line and to operate a full service were calculated to need a minimum share subscription of £625,000. With only £100,000 forthcoming the scheme has been reduced to the running of weekend steam tourist trains over a 3 mile section of the route. This example compares with the £70,000 needed for the Strathspey Railway scheme, some £45,000 of which was raised in three years to pay for acquiring the $5\frac{1}{2}$ mile line and a number of buildings at Aviemore and Boat of Garten. Some of the money came from the 400 supporters, about £20,000 came from loans and £10,000 was a grant from the Highland & Islands Development Board. The latter figure reflects the more helpful attitude now being shown by local authorities and public bodies where a preservation scheme can be seen as an additional local amenity. Private firms too are often generous, but each preservation society must ultimately depend on its own efforts and resources.

As preservationists have gained experience, the early problem of how to run their affairs in a constitutional yet pleasurable way has largely been resolved. The responsibility for owning and operating the line or other asset is normally vested in a conventional limited liability company. This is assisted with finance and voluntary labour by the supporting society whose members may well be shareholders of the operating company and who are also well represented on its board. Other directors usually include major financial supporters, professional advisers, men of prominence in local or railway affairs, and others who will give much of their time and money for the fun they can produce by their labours. The assets of a company may be vested in trustees, and many preservation schemes have qualified for tax advantages by meeting the criteria for

The real work begins after the acquisition of a locomotive: a long, hard task of stripping it down, renewing worn parts, gradually rebuilding and painting. But the end result repays all the effort and cost

being classified as a registered charity. Whatever form of control is appropriate proper accounts must be kept, advisers are needed to handle the legal and technical matters and, of course, enough income has to be generated to cover costs.

In addition to buying its line and buildings, a railway restoration scheme needs a great deal of equipment, be it locomotives and coaches or tickets and timetables. A locomotive may cost several thousand pounds or may come as a gift from a sympathetic firm whose sidings have fallen into disuse. Many main line locomotives have been rescued by small groups of enthusiasts from the Barry scrapyard to which so many displaced BR machines were consigned. The initial cost of, perhaps, £2,000 would be hard enough to raise but hours of labour and many expensive materials will still be required before the engine passes its official boiler test and is ready to go into service. But this is all part of the thrill of preservation, whether it is expressed in locomotive ownership, negotiating with BR and a friendly lorry driver to secure redundant track materials, or hunting down an historic coach body and persuading the owner that he no longer needs it as a summerhouse.

Happily money has been kept in its place in the preservation movement because the work and enthusiasm of the individual supporter compliments the resources, specialist knowledge or business acumen of any patron. Neither patron, skilled operator nor supporter can exist alone, and most railway enthusiasts combine a little of each of these roles. For every pound invested in the movement by a wealthy devotee or sympathetic industry, another has been raised by raffles, sales stalls and the many other devices of amateur fund raising. Subscriptions still only average the price of 100 cigarettes for a year's membership and special rates are usually available for covenanted membership (which gives tax advantages to the society), life membership, young people, senior citizens and families.

Faith and hard work

In return for his subscription to a line preservation activity a supporter can expect a regular magazine or newsletter, the right to influence the affairs of his chosen society, free travel on the trains and strong encouragement to work on the line. Volunteer labour is vital to most lines for even after the route has been acquired and restored to a standard of operational safety high enough to justify the Inspecting Officer of Railways approving the issue of a Light Railway Order, the costs of running trains and maintaining the line in good order are high. Since heavy repairs on a locomotive can cost up to £20,000 it is not surprising that by the time the expense of fuel has been met and the full time staff paid, train working costs can easily reach £3 per mile. Even with 150,000 passengers producing receipts of £30,000 annually a great deal of reliance must still be placed on the financial support of backing groups and the labour of society members.

Of course, not everyone can be an engine driver or a member of the regular operating staff. Indeed, although firing a locomotive is great fun, the task of shovelling coal from a swaying tender to just the right spot in the firebox or bearing the driver's curses and having to rake out the clinker from a dirty fire, is one best savoured occasionally with a few quieter moments collecting car parking charges to give the aching muscles a chance to recover. Even though operating opportunities may be limited most lines need as much help as they can get with track

Restoring a line also means hard, grinding work. Here the Railway Preservation Society's Planet diesel stands on an engineer's train while the 1881 hand crane is used for track repairs

maintenance, repainting and general repair work. Carrying out jobs of this sort is usually well organised, with the operating company planning what needs to be done, providing the necessary equipment and supervision and planning for the refreshment and accommodation of the volunteers.

After this it is up to the individual to enjoy doing a worthwhile job in the company of kindred spirits, but there is no doubt about how good a cup of tea tastes after relaying a length of track, repainting a signal post or repairing the station roof. Other skills, less obvious but equally important, are also required. In addition to selling tickets or refreshments, there is always a demand for people to write newsletters, collect membership fees, run a sales stall at an exhibition or rally or just address envelopes. Others are needed to liaise with local authorities and traders and help with publicity matters, to interest excursion organisers in a visit or to talk to the local bus company about feeder services. There is also the highly complicated world of legislation and the intricacies of finance and accounting, all areas in which professional help is of great assistance.

Where and what to join

Deciding what preservation society you should join warrants some thought, since the evaporation of initial enthusiasm is good for neither the individual nor the society you have chosen. A lot must depend on your interests, but the choice is wide. There are many lines where you can join in an established operational activity and others where you can have the fun of starting from scratch in saving anything from a lamp to a line or locomotive. A number of specialist societies cater for interests in individual railways, special types of preservation and special types of activity, such as the Hull & Barnsley Railway Stock Fund. Societies such as the Dean Forest Railway Preservation Society provide a good example of catering for a wide variety of interests in return for a single subscription. It is preparing to save the freight-only line from Lydney to Parkend in Gloucestershire and can offer restoration work and steam open days at its Parkend premises. More work is going on at a second site at Norchard which will have an operational line before the main scheme is realised. From time to time rail tours are organised to the line and the train which has brought the visitors is used to provide a shuttle service over the route planned for preservation. In winter conventional society

This very professional display in the Great Western Railway Museum, Swindon, gives a good idea of the immense variety of small items held in municipal and similar museums.

activities are available, while the more active can repair fences or reprint the display notices in the museum.

In addition to fulfilling your own recreational and other interests through membership of a railway preservation society, you will soon want to know more about the hobby's overall development and plans. In this sphere a major role is played by the *Association of Railway Preservation Societies*, whose aims are to further the mutual co-operation of preservation bodies and encourage a high standard in the organisation of preservation schemes. Its work has included negotiations to permit private steam locomotives to operate on BR lines, the dissemination of information and advice, the development of codes of practice and many other activities designed to co-ordinate preservation without constraining it. The Association's *Year Book* provides a comprehensive picture of the various societies and what they do and, together with the *Railway & Steam Enthusiasts' Handbook*, should give a prospective preservationist all the information he needs. One other major body is the *Transport Trust* which exists 'to promote the preservation, for the benefit of the nation, of transport items of historical and technical interest'.

5 Trains, Track, and Signals

Since the end product of the railway activity is the train and its most spectacular feature is the locomotive, it is not surprising that trains and traction have always meant much to both practising railwaymen and those who have made railways their hobby. Throughout its history the train has responded in terms of technical design, carrying characteristics and speed to the demands of its environment, and the evolution of the train, from the string of tub wagons on the early colliery tramways to today's Advanced Passenger Train, mirrors the evolution of the nation. The free enterprise doctrines which prevailed during the formative years of the railway system resulted in many imperfections but they also produced a superb variety of trains, ranging from the broad-gauge expresses on the early Great Western lines and the dramatic streamlined trains of the London & North Eastern Railway to the bumbling branch line mixtures and the plodding strings of coal empties returning behind a tired locomotive to the collieries of Yorkshire and South Wales.

When the historic public services commenced on the Stockton & Darlington Railway in 1825, the trains retained many influences from the road vehicles they were soon to displace and provided for private carriages to be driven onto flat wagons for haulage. Open carriages for third and fourth class passengers persisted for some years while the early companies struggled to pay a dividend on the high costs of getting their route authorised and built and of fighting off or buying up competing schemes. Legislation on standards of safety, comfort and charging brought some restraint to the lively activities of the pioneering years and the major companies that were emerging as a result of success, amalgamation or acquisition set about wooing passengers with the comfort of six-wheeled and even bogie carriages and relieving the canals of their freight business by faster services and intensive canvassing.

At first passenger traffic was considered more important than freight. Exciting battles such as the races on the East and West Coast routes to Scotland produced first lighter and faster trains and then bigger locomotives and sumptuous corridor vehicles; the older six-wheel coaches were relegated to slower trains and the mixed passenger and freight services that carried branch line farmers and their livestock to market. The Railways Act of 1921 reduced the 20 or so major companies to four; the areas of competition became fewer but more clearly defined; but still the trains of the Great Western and Southern railways reflected their attempts to secure the lion's share of the Devon and Cornwall traffic. The attractions of rival routes to the Continent and even rival resorts were extolled in some excellent examples of the publicist's art. These years between the two wars produced not only prestige passenger trains and fast freight services designed to ward off growing road competition, but also a wealth of posters, brochures and other literature describing the named services and their attractions and providing yet another area of interest for the enthusiast.

The passenger train services of today comprise main line trains, multiple unit and suburban trains, and special purpose trains. Except on the Southern Region which is electrified on the third rail principle, main line trains are hauled either by diesel locomotives or, on the London Midland Region main line out of Euston, by electric locomotives using a 25kV ac overhead current supply. After a great deal of research at the BR research centre at Derby and a period of testing prototypes, a series of BR standard coach designs evolved into today's 100mph air conditioned stock. The 125mph diesel powered High Speed Train has also started operating on the Western Region and the experimental gas turbine Advanced Passenger Train has already shown its ability to attain its planned operational speed of 150mph. Secondary trains and routes still use older coaches with vacuum brakes instead of air brakes and with steam forcing its way through half frozen pipes instead of electric heating. Some older vehicles still display such interesting features as a label describing the variety of exotic wood used in panelling the compartment, and removable compartment tables.

Electric and diesel

Electric suburban services have been operating for many years, not only on the London Transport and SR networks, but also into Broad Street, Liverpool and Manchester and on the pre-war LNER Wath and Shenfield electrification schemes. The latter used a 1,500 volt dc overhead system before conversion when the rest of the Liverpool Street suburban services were electrified on the mixed 25 and 6.25kV ac system which was evolved to cope with low tunnel clearances. This system was also adopted for the Glasgow and Fenchurch Street electrification schemes leaving all the other services (except the Manchester ones) on the older 630 – 850 volt dc third rail principle. The days of the Liverpool Street steam suburban service with its miracles of intensive signalling, running and station operation and of the Kings Cross quad-art sets of four coaches on five bogies have given way to the electric trains and diesel multiple units although a few examples of the special high-capacity vehicles used for outer suburban services can still be found.

Diesel multiple units, 'dmus' for short, operate in various multiples from one car upwards although the most common combination is that of two under-floor engine power cars and one intermediate vehicle. They appear similar in design but, in fact, represent a variety of coachwork and power unit manufacturers and designs, some even including buffet sections. In addition to suburban services, they operate quite lengthy routes such as the 175 miles from Birmingham to Norwich, and have not only given good and reliable service but have provided the enthusiast with a welcome opportunity to see the line ahead and study the art of driving a machine with an epicyclic gearbox. The dmu's smaller sister, the railbus, was a last attempt to save some branch lines but examples now only remain on a few preserved lines such as the Keighley & Worth Valley Light Railway. The Great Western Society and others have examples of the pioneer GWR railcars but their predecessors, the Sentinel steam railcars, have long since disappeared.

Special trains

Special trains and services are still fairly numerous although excursions were much reduced when BR calculated just how many coaches it was keeping merely to operate such trains and the summer Saturday holiday services. Anglers' and hop pickers' specials have also disappeared; no horse boxes run as 'swingers' behind the Newmarket and Newbury race specials; and the Aberdeen fish train, also classed as a passenger-type service, has lost the battle with road transport. Even trains for royalty, once attended by the glorious paraphernalia of clearing the line and polishing up not only the 'royal' engine but also the reserve locomotives, have declined in numbers and ceremonial.

In their place have come services like the Motorail network with trains consisting of passenger, refreshment and sometimes sleeping vehicles followed by a set of car wagons. The range of sleeper services is also exten-

Unsung efficiency. Just an ordinary 'long goods train' to the layman, this Class 7 air-braked 'Merry-go-round' coal train is preparing to circle Didcot power station, discharge its coal, and leave without having stopped

sive and will carry the traveller overnight from Euston to Inverness or Bristol to Edinburgh; the modernised parcels train network demonstrates the functional end. This highly sophisticated facility uses 'Brute' (British Railways Universal Trolley Equipment) trucks which are filled with parcels for a particular destination and then loaded into the special vans of parcels trains operating to a regular pattern between main stations and transhipment points.

Hauling the freight

The variety of freight trains is as great as that of passenger trains. For many years the majority of wagons were owned by the firms forwarding the traffic but in later years wagons for general goods, steel and livestock were provided by the railways leaving the coal and mineral wagons to be provided by private companies. Until road competition made itself felt, freight trains were planned to achieve large loads rather than high speeds but in an endeavour to meet the challenge of the lorry a whole range of express freight trains was developed, tightly timed, often named and all using at least a proportion of wagons fitted with vacuum brakes and screw couplings, in contrast to the unbraked wagons of the early years. Despite these efforts and the extensive use of containers which were collected and delivered to and from the trains by road vehicles, railways carried less and less freight. Raising rates and cutting the wagon fleet produced a further decline until a new concept was ushered in during the 1960s, based on running whole train loads instead of the single wagons which lost so much time when being transferred from one train to another at marshalling yards.

The block train load concept started with an agreement with the oil companies to phase out their small 4,000 gallon tank wagons and replace them with 1,000 ton trains of much larger wagons running straight from the refineries to tank farms in the using areas. The final local deliveries were then performed by road vehicles. The system was extended to cement traffic and now embraces stone, milk, fertilisers and many other commodities. Ford cars were the first prestige commodity to pass in train loads, first in covered vans, then on Carflat wagons and now on privately-owned wagons with wheels small enough to permit two tiers of vehicles to be carried within the limited BR loading gauge.

BR also devised a special form of block train load operation for coal traffic. Here the desirability of high wagon utilisation led to the so-called

'Merry-go-Round trains', which load on the move beneath the colliery screens and then set off for power stations equipped with private sidings laid out in a loop. Without stopping, the train passes slowly over the discharge hoppers where levers on the Hop AB wagons are tripped to release their contents and allow the train to head back to the colliery for another load. Many other commodities are the subject of such special systems.

Container freight

The railways revived their interests in the general haulage market with the development of the Freightliner network which involves specially designed low wagons operating in regular train patterns carrying both Freightliner and privately owned containers. Huge transfer cranes can be seen lifting the containers between trains and road vehicles at such main centres as London (Stratford, Willesden, Barking and Tilbury), Manchester (Longsight and Old Trafford), Liverpool, Edinburgh and Glasgow. Passengers travelling westwards from Southampton can see two of these terminals from the train, the Millbrook terminal to the north of the line and, to the south, the newer terminal built to deal with maritime traffic to and from the Far East. More recently still a new fast freight service has been developed for general goods. Known as the Air Braked Network, this uses a new design of high capacity ABN van and offers fast transit between selected points. Ordinary freight business is still carried and coal trains are still numerous. Trains of engineer's department wagons are frequently in evidence relaying track, carrying ballast, undertaking maintenance of the overhead electric equipment or working with the ugly, but efficient, Matissa track maintenance machines.

The diesel revolution

Of course, the train would be nothing without the locomotive which has commanded so much interest and admiration since Trevithick produced his original design in 1804. Stephenson's *Rocket*, following a quarter of a century later, produced a much higher heating surface by using a number of tubes in the boiler and started a history of progressive design improvement that has continued ever since.

As locomotives became bigger, frames were provided to support the heavier boiler, the live steam injector replaced the water feed pump actuated by the motion and, in the 1870s, braking by destroying the vacuum that held the brakes off replaced the primitive hand brakes of earlier years. About ten years earlier the Kirtley firebox had permitted a change from coke to coal burning but single driving wheels, gradually getting larger and larger, were the rule for passenger engines for many years and only gave way to 4–4–0 and 4–4–2 designs around the turn of the century. So-called 'Pacific' type locomotives, with a 4–6–2 wheel arrangement of four leading wheels, six coupled driving wheels and two wheels trailing beneath the cab, appeared after World War I on the Great Northern and North Eastern lines and eventually developed to raise the world speed record to 126mph in 1938.

With the many 4–6–0 types, the Pacifics dominated the main line passenger train scene with various smaller designs, compounds and tank engines catering for the secondary services. In the same way 0–6–0 tender and tank designs hauled most freight services for nearly a hundred years although 2–6–0s and 0–8–0s worked some services and a few special designs such as the powerful Lickey incline banking engine and a few articulated locomotives for heavy freight trains were also built.

On nationalisation in 1948 British Railways took over 20,024 steam locomotives and soon determined upon a new building programme based on 12 standard designs. Before the first thousand had been constructed a momentous decision was taken to abandon steam traction, and a range of diesel designs began to appear to join the diesel shunting engines which had been increasing in numbers for some time. With manufacturing capacity swamped by this decision a mixture of engine and body types was inevitable and a number of combinations proved unsatisfactory and were eventually abandoned, including the boldly experimental Warship hydraulic transmission machines. There are now over 30 main types of diesel locomotive dominated by the Class 08 0–6–0 shunters, the Class 24–5 BR/Beyer-Peacock, Class 31 Brush and Class 37 English Electric mixed traffic machines and the Class 47 BR/Brush twelve-wheel designs used on so many passenger trains. In addition there are eleven main types of electric locomotive, including two electro-diesel designs which can use the SR third rail current direct or drive the traction motors by means of a diesel generator.

Commercial publications are available detailing all locomotives, diesel multiple units and types of electric stock. They provide an opportunity to study the many variations that appear within each class and also the various special purpose units such as de-icing vehicles. Each type of

An interesting study in the final age of steam: West Country 'Pacific' 34011 *Tavistock* heads the 'Devon Belle' Pullman out of Okehampton in 1949

motive power has a class number which can be exemplified in terms of the diesel locomotives where the higher the number, the higher the power group of the machine. Thus Class 01 represents the two 153bhp Barclay shunters, and Class 55 the powerful English Electric Deltic class which covers so many miles on the East Coast main line. The class number also forms the first two digits of the locomotive number, beneath which is carried a plate giving information for use in traffic working, especially when the locomotive is not operating to its normal diagram.

The data embraces the weight of the locomotive which is important when passing over bridges and similar structures, the brake force which is used as part of a system which calculates the running characteristics of vehicles and translates these into a safe braking power requirement, and a route code which denotes the ability or otherwise to negotiate curves or other restrictions on any given route – the bigger the locomotive, the higher the number and the lower the ability to negotiate difficult routes. On the front of the locomotive the head-code showed, until recently, the type of train, its destination and its train number.

The first carriages

Conditioned by the highway tradition of private carriages, stage coaches and the lumbering wagon used by the less wealthy, a tradition perpetuated by the canal passenger boats, the early railways provided flat trucks on which private carriages could be mounted and carried the impecunious in unadorned open wagons. Slowly the former became an integral chassis and coach body and the latter acquired, in stages, seats, a roof and then windows.

Progress was erratic and standards differed greatly even within the same company. The Great Western, for example, provided excellent first and second class facilities but treated its poorer patrons in a decidedly cavalier fashion. Competition tended to influence standards more than legislation, and although the Regulation of Railways Act of 1844 required all companies to provide third class passengers with at least one train a day of reasonable comfort, costing not more than one penny per mile and running no slower than 12mph, most railways responded either by running such trains when no one wanted to travel or by taking the vehicles that would not meet the standards of the Act and creating a fourth class with them.

Improvements started to come as the railway network stabilised. By the 1860s lighting by oil pot was giving way to gas lamps, with bogie vehicles appearing on the Great Northern and Midland main lines a few years later. Then the Midland went further and, by abolishing second class, made the horsehair seats of former second class vehicles available to third class passengers. Soon standards were rising steadily, with the hardy days of meal stops and foot warmers giving way to an era of well-lit coaches, many provided with corridors and lavatories and some trains including dining and sleeping vehicles.

Development did not follow a regular pattern. Six-wheelers were still nearly universal on the North British Railway's lines when the Brighton Pullman coaches reached 60ft long, only slightly shorter than today's standard vehicle. Nevertheless, the terrible fire hazard of gas-lit wooden vehicles gradually disappeared as electric lighting was taken from axle-driven dynamos and steel frames became universal. With its clipper-built body, semi-elliptical roof and quality finish, the main line coaching vehicle had reached a high standard by the time the railways were nationalised. However, due to the wartime scarcity of materials many older coaches remained at work long after they would normally have been scrapped – but this helped to enrich the preservation scene when new, all-steel vehicles eventually took over.

Excellent books have been written on the history of the railway carriage, the forms it took and the liveries and embellishments with which it was adorned, and many examples can still be seen among the collections of the railway museums and preservation centres. The National Railway Museum at York, for example, features two 1834 vehicles from the Bodmin & Wadebridge Railway as well as later and more extravagant designs. Most of the standard-gauge preserved lines have examples of stock from the 'Big Four' companies and the Bluebell Railway collection also includes items from the lines which were grouped as the Southern Railway.

Lines such as the Dart Valley give an insight into the variety of stock operated by an individual company. Among its passenger vehicles it includes not only the commonplace open third class coaches and the auto trailers used on trains which could be driven from either end, but also the super saloons of the Plymouth expresses and a saloon used by the directors for making their tours of inspection. Former GWR freight stock on the railway is equally varied, with banana vans and insulated vans mingling with ordinary open and covered wagons, and tank and bogie bolster wagons representing the sphere of specialised traffics. Departmental vehicles include an engineer's inspection saloon, a dynamometer car, a breakdown tool van and a shunters' truck.

Coaching stock in use today is still varied and interesting. On the older vehicles a metal plate at the ends records the main dimensions and the lighting is still generated from the rotation of the axles. Bogies of differing designs are numerous, and a loose coach may still be spotted to reveal the heavy 'buckeye' clasp coupling, the flexible steam and vacuum brake pipes and the awkward 'concertina' shields. Modern formations, joined and separated less often than in the days of multi-portion trains and slip coaches, are much simpler in this respect but more complicated in other ways, especially with the introduction of the Mark IIE coaches which are air conditioned and have a public address system.

In these vehicles the thermostatic air conditioning unit uses an evaporator for cooling, electric elements for heating, and grilles, ducts and filters for the ventilating process. Power is taken from the locomotive at 800 volts and, by means of an alternator on each coach, provides a low voltage supply for lighting and for charging the emergency battery and a 415 volt ac supply for the other functions. Coach markings include the legend Inter City and the vehicle number and owning region on the

Typical of the observation cars used on prestige trains through scenic areas. This is a car from the SR 'Devon Belle' Pullman, seen behind GWR 0–4–2T 1420 crossing Nursery Pool Bridge on the Dart Valley Railway

side, with inspection dates on the main frame member below or at the vestibule end. Here too are details of the maximum speed, the route restriction code, the heating and braking methods and a vehicle type code. Evolved for stock reporting in the days of the morse telegraph system this is not difficult to interpret as FO stands for First (class) Open (as opposed to corridor) vehicle, SK for a Second Corridor coach, BCK for Brake Composite (of first and second class) Corridor and so on. Colour symbols on multiple units denote which vehicles may be coupled together.

For years the railway wagon was essentially an open, planked body on a four-wheel metal frame, with axles revolving in a grease-filled box and with only the lever handbrake for braking. A train with flapping wagon sheets, a smoking 'hot box' and bouncing brake levers was a common sight well into the 1950s. In addition to covered vans and cattle wagons there was a fleet of 1 ton (A), 4 ton (B, BD and BK) and other containers to provide door to door conveyance without the goods being transhipped at the station goods shed, but most other vehicles were coal and mineral wagons largely provided by the users and bearing their names.

Until the system was unified, the Railway Clearing House was kept busy apportioning earnings and costs to match the exchange of wagons from one system to another and had an army of numbertakers to record the data on which this was based. With the need for increasing speeds came the XP goods van, fitted with vacuum brakes worked from the engine or at least carrying the vacuum pipe to enable it to make up the unbraked portion of 'partially fitted' express freight trains. All wagons on the various categories of fast freight service had screw couplings in place of the three-link loose coupling which allowed the locomotive of a slow, heavy train to take the strain of the load gradually. Fitted and unfitted brake vans are now rare as the train guard normally rides on the locomotive and most of the fruit, fish, gunpowder and other special wagons have gone, but others have replaced them and the standard 10ft wheelbase goods van is still commonplace.

Freight vehicle trends

The main changes in freight vehicles in recent years have been the dramatic reduction in numbers and the steady increase in capacity, from the former 10–12 tons to the 16–32 ton range of the mineral wagon and the 20,000 gallon, 72½ ton load of a typical modern, privately-owned tank wagon. The evolution of new types of specialised wagon has not been confined to the stone hoppers, tanks and other designs of the private owner but has included Palvans built by BR to handle pallet traffic, shock absorbing wagons for bricks, ferry vans for European traffic and the 35 ton vans for the Air Braked Network. Plate, tube and bogie bolster wagons carried steel traffic for many years but were then joined by hooded steel wagons, and then well wagons evolved to carry the increasing proportion of steel produced in coil form. The Freightliner wagons are distinctive and have disc brakes, twistlocks to hold the containers in position and a light but strong form of construction that enables them to carry containers in multiples of 10, 20, 30 and 40ft.

Parcels traffic was traditionally carried by passenger trains but these are now largely reserved for mail and urgent Red Star parcels. Other traffic has a system of its own which evolved from a sorting method based on a destination code and has now become a highly disciplined network using dedicated vehicles and equipment. Parcels collected or handed in at stations are loaded into the Brute cage trucks and towed to the trains by small, battery-powered tractors. The standard formation parcels trains then move the traffic to a timetabled service using BGV (Brake Van Gangway), GUV (General Utility Van), CCT (Covered Carriage Truck) and other such vehicles.

Local parcels workings and such special services as those carrying Cornish broccoli and flowers from the Isles of Scilly draw from a mixed fleet which includes Siphon vehicles, some LMR vans still fitted with ogee windows to allow the guard to see along the line, some 4 and 6-wheel trucks, many with their own peculiarities such as the narrow door handles of former SR stock. The activity includes extensive road vehicle movements and transfers, has purpose-built sorting centres such as that at Peterborough and is closely linked with the GPO activity.

Some rare items can be found among the departmental vehicles including a few Chapman weedkilling vans and an occasional Pooley weighing machine testing van, although the latter have decreased rapidly since the days when most stations had a weighing machine, a cart weighbridge or even a wagon weighbridge. The engineers use a delightful collection of vehicles for carrying and distributing ballast and rails, each bearing the name of a sea creature. Further variety is added to the vehicle fleet by the trucks of Taunton concrete works, the snowploughs like the one in Crewe south yard, the Enpart vans distributing locomotive spares to and from Swindon, the red riding and equipment vans of a breakdown train, the electrification foundation drilling, mast-erecting and wiring trains, tunnel inspection vehicles, and many others.

The railway devotee will be well rewarded for turning away from trains long enough to examine the other railway equipment. To get a passenger on a train requires posters and pamphlets, ticket and enquiry offices, the large Multiprinter and Flexiprinter ticket machines, as well as some Setright issuing machines for conductor guards, and a few surviving examples of the old Edmonson card tickets with racks to supply them and dating machines to validate them. Seats, barrows, waiting rooms, buffets, even hotels and ships, support the passenger activity, while freight has the road collection and delivery services and items as large as a gantry crane or fork lift truck and as small as a shunting pole or Bardic handlamp.

Variety has given way to clarity in station signs but the architecture and ironwork may still reveal gargoyled window arches at Crewe or the superb roof support systems at Paddington and Carlisle. Most large stations and carriage depots have a Britannia carriage washing plant, but brake sticks for manually braking wagons and wooden 'sprags' for placing through the axle bracket and wheel spokes to hold a wagon are much rarer. Whether it be a manual indicator board, a time-honoured clock or a Brute loading board there is still much to see on the railway system for the keen and interested observer.

On and By the Line

The early tramways were simple affairs, and for track used crude wooden rails laid upon stone blocks and held together by cross ties. The first metal rails were L-shaped, George Stephenson devising the edge rail system with the restraining flange transferred to the vehicle wheels as one of his innovations for the Stockton & Darlington Railway. *Permanent way*, so called to distinguish it from the temporary track used by the contractors building a railway, varied considerably from line to line in the early years for there was no code of practice to lean on and the right answers emerged from putting sound engineering instincts to the test of practical usage.

On the section between London and Maidenhead the GWR initially used rails weighing 43lb per yard laid on longitudinal timbers 14in wide by 7in deep and with transoms and strap bolts. Heavier rails of 62lb per

This major bridge renewal job calls for civil engineering equipment and skills, two high-capacity cranes and four different freight vehicles, among them a bogie bolster wagon and two former container flat (Conflat) wagons

yard were soon substituted but by 1843 the line had again been relaid, this time with 75lb track. Eventually common standards were adopted by most companies and based upon 95lb 'bullhead' rails held in metal chairs on each sleeper by oaken keys and bolted together by fishplates. Recent years have seen the introduction first of flat-bottomed rails and then of continuous welded rail capable of absorbing its own expansion and giving a much smoother ride than bullhead track, although the latter remains fairly common on secondary and lower graded lines and sidings where the chairs still occasionally bear the initials of near-forgotten companies.

The construction era was a colourful one well described in Terry Coleman's book *The Railway Navvies*. Aided only by picks and shovels, barrows and horses, the itinerant 'navigators' achieved the same prodigious feats in constructing the railways that they had shown in the canal building era, responding, in the worst of conditions, to foremen and engineers who were as tough as themselves and had learned their new science in the hard school of experience.

Like roads and canals, railways cost least where they could follow contour lines and avoid rivers and other physical obstacles, but this produced longer routes which were more expensive to operate. The poorer companies frequently had to accept this situation but bigger schemes were routed as directly as the trains of the day could work. Engineers were expected to keep costs down by exercising their skill and ingenuity. The system produced some great engineers; it used a community of hard working, hard living labourers with their own brand of comradeship and social problems, and it created a wide variety of routes of varying degrees of distinction. It is still possible to note how the soil from a cutting was used to form an embankment, how the course of a valley or canal was exploited, and to see how the compromise between directness and cost was resolved, although many sharp gradients and curves have since been eased and traffic transferred from poor routes to better ones.

Which rail gauge?

The biggest debate of the early years was over the ideal gauge. The Eastern Counties Railway briefly chose 5ft but all the other main lines built to 4ft 8½in with the exception of the GWR with its visionary 7ft 0¼in-gauge. A gauge war developed, with the GWR and its adjoining rivals each trying to persuade new companies to adopt their gauge. Matters worsened as the companies grew and traffic had to be transferred manually between the wagons of the two systems except on routes where a third rail was laid between the broad gauge ones. The arguments between the stability of the Brunel line and the economy of the standard gauge ended in an historic Parliamentary examination and the GWR having to undertake the massive task of conversion. Today the GWR lines still have a spaciousness that is the envy of those routing out-of-gauge loads.

Some physical obstacles could not be avoided by the railway builders. Pride of place among the tunnels which resulted goes to the 4.4 mile tunnel beneath the Severn on the GWR main line to South Wales, where the 25 million gallons a day from the Great Spring that broke into the original workings still has to be contained by giant electric pumps. On the same line is the 2.5 mile Sodbury tunnel between Badminton and Chipping Sodbury while just a few miles to the south, on the main line to Bristol, lies Box tunnel through whose 1.1 miles the sun is said to shine only on Brunel's birthday. Another group of long British tunnels involves the Pennine range whose lofty and beautiful peaks separate some of Britain's major industrial conglomerations and the markets they serve. On each east to west route at least one major tunnel was unavoidable. The Midland Railway, needing access to Manchester from its London to Sheffield main line, chose Totley for a 3.5 mile engineering masterpiece and then had to bore another 2.1 miles at Cowburn just before meeting the now-truncated line from Derby which had its own tunnel at Doves Hole. Another 2.2 mile tunnel was necessary at Disley to make this a costly piece of railway. The other two major Pennine tunnels, Woodhead on the Great Central's Penistone route and Standedge on the London & North Western line from Manchester to Huddersfield, both exceed 3 miles in length.

To travel through a tunnel on the footplate of a steam engine, with only the darting orange glow of the firebox to light the shadows of the enginemen and give substance to the rushing walls, was a memorable experience. Today, without the exhaust smoke blowing back from a dirty fire, it is still exciting to plunge into the 2.1 miles of tunnel at Bramhope on the Leeds–Harrogate line, to burst from the 2.2 miles of tunnel at Roman Bridge upon the slate world of Blaenau Ffestiniog or to pass through any of the two dozen long tunnels still open – all very simple to the passenger but all a constant challenge to the maintenance skills of the civil engineers and the working care and emergency precautions of the operating department.

The challenge of bridges

Railway bridges, too, repay study. The 11,653ft lattice girder bridge across the Tay at Dundee is not only the longest in the United Kingdom but also has the most dramatic history. It was here, on a wild night just after Christmas in 1879, that the first bridge collapsed and drowned a whole trainload of people in the waters of the Firth below. The neighbouring structure across the Forth between Dalmeny and North Queensferry is not as long, but its triple cantilever design makes it equally notable. Further north, on the lonely Highland Railway route to Inverness, the red sandstone arches across Culloden Moor are equally impressive in a different way. Robert Stephenson's bridges across the Menai Strait, over the Tyne at Newcastle and linking England and Scotland over the Tweed at Berwick are not only bridges of stature in their own right but show the variety of approach of which this early railway engineer was capable. The imaginative will also marvel at Brunel's Royal Albert Bridge across the Tamar where not the least of the constructional problems was floating the tubular piers into position and anchoring them there. Many other types of bridge can still be found, from the high level bridge at Newcastle which carries both road and rail traffic to the swing bridges over the waterways of East Anglia – all exhibiting something of interest if only in the ornamentation of the ironwork or the origins of the building materials.

Topping the heights

The highest summit lies between Perth and Inverness where even 'The Clansman' takes 168 minutes to cover the wild and beautiful 117.75 miles through Blair Atholl and the ski centre of Aviemore to reach the northern capital. Just north of Dalnaspidal, after 16 miles of gruelling gradients of 1 foot rise in 70 and 1 in 85, comes the summit at Druimuachdar, 1,484ft above sea level, to be followed beyond Carr Bridge by Slochd Summit and then 22½ miles of rushing downgrades into Inver-

Shap Summit, the famous high altitude point, before electrification. The special engineering train is preparing foundations for the overhead power masts. Note the upper quadrant signal and facing points mechanism

ness. Further west on the West Highland route to Fort William and Mallaig lie the Corrour and Tyndrum summits to add thrills to this wild and lonely line as it curves over Rannoch Moor and by Loch Treig before dropping down into Fort William. On the West Coast route to Scotland the summits at Shap and Beattock have always been names to conjure with, but at least the alignment is reasonably straight and the freight locomotiveman's problem was the straightforward one of enough steam going up and enough braking power coming down.

This difficulty showed up starkly on the competing route of the Midland Railway over the lonely fells and through Appleby. At Aisgill summit on the night of 2 September 1913 a southbound sleeping car train stalled on the 1 in 100 gradient and the following driver, steaming hard to lift his train over the daunting rise, misread the signals and crashed into the first train to cause a disastrous fire and many casualties. Further south the Pennines produce gradients as well as tunnels, and the West Midlands has the notable Lickey incline of 1 in 37.75 for 2 miles. In the steam era up to three 'banking' engines might be needed to assist northbound freight trains and some rear assistance still takes place. The other lines all had notable gradients such as the speed stretch of Stoke Bank south of Grantham (where two world records were created), the Great Western's four heavy gradients in South Devon, and the good running portion of the London & South Western Railway near Honiton.

Lineside gradient posts mark these locations and denote the number of feet in which the route rises or falls one foot. There may also be catch points to derail runaway trains and notices requiring drivers to pin down a number of wagon brakes. Mileposts record the distances in round numbers with the method of showing the quarter miles varying according to the original company. Distances normally count from London or a main line junction and trains to London or certain former company headquarters stations are Up trains. Speed limits, the yellow boards and white figures denoting permanent way restrictions, and 'Whistle' signs all give guidance to drivers, while other lineside furniture includes platelayers huts, trespass warnings, structure number plates, farm crossings and many other items.

Switches and junctions

Track not only varies in standard according to the traffic using it but may also range from single lines to highly complex junctions which involve double leads, switch diamonds and other special rail formations. Single lines of any length are usually provided with passing loops but, even so, their lower cost has to be reckoned against their lower carrying capacity. The capacity of double lines can be increased by using 'refuge' sidings whose points 'trail' into the running line in the direction of travel and which allow a fast train to pass a slow one. Loops perform a similar function and where their entry and exit points are controlled by different signal boxes they become goods or slow lines. Here too company practice differed, the GWR grouping its Up and Down Slow lines together but the LNER placing them outside its fast lines.

The main line out of King's Cross provides some good examples of the various types of track, starting with a most complicated system of track and points to get an Up train across all the other lines to the suburban station on the opposite side of the complex. Tunnels follow in fairly rapid succession all the way to Potters Bar, with the first few miles also producing examples of not only fast and slow lines but also goods and permissive lines, carriage sidings and flyover bridges. There is also a maintenance depot at Finsbury Park, a freight marshalling yard at Ferme Park, carriage sidings at Wood Green and, further north, the lofty Welwyn viaduct and more tunnels.

The maintenance of all this track is a complicated and skilled task. The continuous welded rail now used on most main lines is laid from special engineer's trains rather like an obstinate, ungainly cable, but the less spectacular work on other lines and the adjusting processes of 'top and line' or correcting 'creep' and 'cant' is still done by the ganger and his lengthmen tamping just the right amount of ballast under just the right sleeper. Most of the routine work on the heavily used lines is now done mechanically using a fascinating collection of Matissa machines, which spend their nights and weekends cleaning, tamping, fettling or gauging so that the track lies true and its ballast provides a firm bed which will drain well and even out the stress on the wooden or concrete sleepers.

The BR civil engineering function also covers buildings and land. Much surplus property has, in fact, been disposed of in recent years, but some good examples of station goods sheds remain and the fading legend 'LMS Grain Warehouse No 2' carried on a typical railway warehouse at Burton-on-Trent is a reminder of the huge grain business once carried by the railways and the department devoted to hiring out sacks for it. Many stations have been rebuilt or rationalised, outstanding examples being Birmingham New Street and Euston. Also in London, King's Cross has recently been restyled rather than rebuilt, while Liverpool Street and Broad Street are the subject of a proposed scheme for combination and simplification. Many reminders of past grandeur exist, none more splendid than the facade of St Pancras. By comparison Cambridge appears quite doleful, but to compensate it has the unusual single main platform with the double crossover which allows the ends to be used by trains proceeding in opposite directions. Some of the smaller stations that have been modernised are now quite austere while other schemes have produced an unhappy mixture of old and new, as at Peterborough where straightening out the original curve has virtually marooned the main station buildings. However, stations like York and Bristol remain as imposing as ever and there is still plenty of character to be found at such places as Great Malvern and Windsor, where the old railway structures are still giving good service in a modern setting.

Signalling and Operation

For the earliest of trains, proceeding slowly and in daylight, an interval between departures and a good lookout by the driver was sufficient for safety. However, with train sizes and speeds increasing much faster than braking capacity, the need for some form of control system quickly became evident. Signalmen are still known as 'Bobbies' as a result of this duty being allocated to the early railway policemen, who held one arm straight out to signify a safe interval since the passage of the previous train, raised the arm to recommend caution and held up both arms to require a train to stop. Visibility limitations, especially in poor light, led to the use of mechanical signals and oil lamps with coloured glasses, where a bar or disc would show against a train to restrain its progress and where red indicated stop, green caution and white clear. Points were worked separately.

A round of more sophisticated development began in 1841 with the advent of the first inclined-arm semaphore signals and the introduction of Cooke & Wheatstone's electric telegraph to control train working through the North Midland Railway's Clay Cross Tunnel. Slowly the control of points was grouped with that of the signals protecting them, and in 1856 John Saxby patented his system of interlocking the two so that the signal indication always reflected the position of the points. Pro-

An ordinary station scene? Lineside features around the south end of Bristol (Temple Meads) include the lights, breakdown crane and water tank of the motive power unit, colour light signals, relay boxes and a speed restriction sign

gress was neither uniform nor fast enough and accidents were all too frequent, especially before the passing of the Regulation of Railways Act 1889. This made compulsory the block working system, the interlocking of points and signals and the provision of automatic brakes on passenger trains. After this, railway safety improved steadily as the problems of weather, mechanical failure and human fallibility were met, investigated, and slowly overcome.

Although electric working of points and signals began before the turn of the century, uniformity of practice, even with the traditional manual operation of signal boxes, was slow to come. The GWR stuck to its lower quadrant arms long after the other companies had chosen upper quadrant signals, which had the force of gravity as well as a counterweight to return them to danger if a signal wire broke, and parts of the LNER used 'somersault' signals pivoted in the middle of the arm until relatively recent times.

A big step forward in standardisation followed a disastrous collision at

Welwyn in 1935, the resultant accident investigation by the Ministry of Transport's Inspecting Officer of Railways leading to the general adoption of the so-called Welwyn Block system which still holds good in principle today. Except on 'permissive' lines, where goods trains are admitted under special cautions, standard block signalling permits only one train to be in a section, requires that the section be proved clear before the train is admitted and maintains ahead an adequate braking distance — traditionally a quarter of a mile.

A basic signalling 'section' has distant, home and starter signals, on each line and in that order, with the latter controlling the entrance to the next section and not lowered until the signalman there has received from the signalman ahead a visual telegraphic 'Train Out of Section' clearance for the previous train and 'Line Clear' on the Block Instruments, after requesting permission by means of a bell code, for the passage of the next train. The other main feature of basic signalling is the use of low voltage track circuits whose interruption by the passage of a train not only records its progress visually on the track diagram in the signal box, but is

No 9 *Prince of Wales* leaves Aberystwyth on British Rail's only narrow-gauge line, watched by a railwayman in the old-style heavy uniform, who is standing by to operate the points from the ground frame

also used in the complicated interlocking arrangements which prevent conflicting signals being cleared.

Signals: semaphore and lights

Despite the modernisation schemes of recent years, the traditional semaphore signal can still be seen in numbers protecting points, junctions, level crossings and sidings. Such signals usually stand to the left of the line to which they refer and use a red arm (and red light) in the horizontal position to indicate stop and a yellow 'fishtail' arm on the distance signals to require caution because the next signal is at 'danger'. The reverse side is white and black with a white light and masking disc, although this device for enabling the signalman to check the aspect of his signals at night may be supplemented by a 'repeater' instrument in the signal box.

In their simplest form running line signals, and the slightly smaller shunting and calling-on signals, are pulled to the 45° upper quadrant 'off' position by a system of wires and balance weights connected to the signal box lever frame.

Points may still be worked by a system of rods, and those lying in the facing direction on a running line have a bar device to lock them home and a slotted tie rod to verify this. Movements through local points may be protected by ground signals. The same equipment was, and still is, used on single lines but here a special staff, tablet or token, withdrawn from a machine that is interlocked with the signals and block instruments, constitutes an additional authority to use the line. Ground frames are used to control local points some distance from the signal box and cannot be operated until the signalman has released them by a method which then prevents him from allowing a conflicting movement. Away from running lines points are changed by means of a hand lever and shunting controlled by hand and lamp movements.

The newly-formed Southern Railway, with its dense suburban traffic, gave a boost to the use of electric power for signalling in the 1920s and was the first to introduce colour light signals which increased line capacity by displaying two yellow lights as a preliminary caution. At Newport the GWR introduced the first signal box where all movements were power actuated, and this company also pioneered an automatic train control scheme, predecessor of the present Automatic Warning System, which provides an indication in the locomotive cab of the aspect shown by the signals. Electric route indicators, points motors and other

Modern contrast. The interior of Motherwell panel signal box shows the control panel and the general paraphernalia of train regulating

refinements followed with a further round of major changes originating in the BR Modernisation Plan.

This eventually produced highly sophisticated MAS (Multiple Aspect Signalling) schemes, using electronic remote control based on the miniturisation of relays and other components, to cover nearly half of the railway's 23,000 track miles. Over many of these miles trains protect themselves by actuating signals by their passage and, with the new 'panel' signal boxes able to control routes over much greater distances, many of the older type of signal box have disappeared. The change, which has concentrated the route setting and train code and progress description over many miles upon a single control panel, has also changed the role of the signal box from one of passing and reporting trains to one of traffic regulation.

What signals are for

All this signalling exists to facilitate the safe and rapid passage of trains and their traffic. This is done to a plan which starts, in the case of the passenger service, with an assessment of the travel needs for each line and service and is then followed by a calculation of the approximate number of train 'sets' required. Once a satisfactory compromise is worked out to match these two factors to the amount of equipment available detailed planning can start. The process will use a table of calculated or tested running times and take account of the ruling 'head-way' needed between trains on each route. On a level line with equi-distant colour light signals this ruling headway would be about 2 miles but, with many signals still sited near the stations and junctions they served in the past, the permissible distance between trains varies along the route and the ruling headway becomes, in practice, the greatest such distance.

Using the running times and allowing for the ruling headway, train 'paths' are then compiled, with due allowance for working at stations and for 'turnrounds' – detraining, cleaning, watering, stocking the buffet car and so on – at each terminal, and with some manipulation of the size and weight of the train and the type of locomotive allocated in order to provide for non-standard situations such as very fast trains or the need to attach and detach vehicles en route.

When all the planning compromises have been made, the results are plotted on a graph which bears locations along one axis and times along the other. Here adjustments are made to fit in the paths for the freight and parcels trains and to allow for engine and empty carriage movements before the results can be expressed in the form of area working timetables and, ultimately, in the public timetables. Concurrently the movements of locomotives, coaching stock and train staff will be set out as 'diagrams' which pass to motive power depots, carriage sheds and the other working locations concerned as their basis for supplying the right resources at the right time. A similar process takes place in miniature for special movements and many subsidiary plans are drawn up for peak periods and at the working locations, which must relate available staff to the diagram requirements, inform train announcers, enquiry and operating staff and, after the event, monitor performance, pay wages and cover a hundred other such functions.

The passenger and parcels activity is fairly obvious to the observant traveller but much more of the freight operation takes place at night or away from passenger stations. The traditional pattern was for the local 'pick-up' services to collect loaded traffic each afternoon on the way to the local marshalling yard and leave the empties ordered for loading on the following day. A complex network of overnight services then

Just a line of trucks in a yard? Using gravity, this unattended 'rake' of wagons is passing through the retarders in Whitemoor Down Yard, while another movement is pushed to the top of the hump

exchanged traffic between the marshalling points after some hectic hours sorting and collecting the wagons by flat or hump shunting. In essence this process still occurs, but much more traffic passes in train loads avoiding marshalling yards, the volume of business and the number of goods terminals are both fewer and the TOPS (Total Operations Processing System) data exchange method allows much more pre-planning than was formerly possible.

Some 850 exchange points are provided for in the TOPS code but the majority of these undertake only a limited amount of flat shunting. In this process the shunter reads the wagon label, uncouples as the shunting engine (or 'pilot') starts to move and thus slackens the couplings, and then halts the train so that the uncoupled wagon will continue into the siding previously selected by movement of the hand points. There are some large manual yards, such as the WR's exchange sidings at Acton, and big mechanised yards at such places as Carlisle, Toton, Margam, Temple Mills and Whitemoor. The latter is an early example of a mechanised 'hump' yard in which trains run into the reception sidings and are examined in order to produce a 'cut card' indicating how many wagons are destined for each of the sorting sidings on the other side of the raised hump. The train is then propelled slowly over this, each cut running down the other side with sufficient clearance (caused by the rise of the hump) for the points to be reset between movements which, in turn, have been based upon the cut card information. Power-operated 'retarders' apply a wheel pressure (automatically based on wagon weight and rolling characteristics in some yards) to slow the wagons down again so that they will roll smoothly into the sorting sidings where they are coupled and then drawn onto the departure lines for their forward journey.

Cleaning and maintenance

Many other features go to make up the operating activity of running a railway. Passenger stock not only receives its cleaning and watering between journeys but goes to the carriage sidings for external washing and thorough internal cleaning and to the carriage shops for regular preventative maintenance. Wheels are still tapped for 'flat tyres' and to detect metal flaws. Freight stock and locomotives receive just as much attention and there are highly complex systems to control this. Signalmen and operating staff must pass stringent tests of their operating knowledge, as must drivers and guards. A freight guard must approve the condition of his train before departure, using a train preparation form. This records the weight of each wagon and its load, the braking and route characteristics and the maximum speed (all shown on the wagon) and allows the aggregate to be checked against the brake force, route availability and maximum speed shown on the locomotive, in order to ensure that the train is within its safe and timetabled classification. Wagon types are classified in 'standard wagon lengths' of 21ft so that the length of a train can be calculated and kept within the capacity of any loop or siding into which it may have to be shunted on its journey.

Safety first

Railwaymen have an ingrained tradition of maintaining safety but despite the stringent regulations and sophisticated equipment, emergencies of abnormal traffic or accident conditions can arise. A control organisation works in conjunction with signalmen and station staff to handle the missed connections and other complications of late running, to deal with other unscheduled incidents − which range from storm damage to cows on the line − and to provide for safety, rescue and line clearance in the event of an emergency. The mechanical failure of a loco-motive may appear a simple matter, but even after a fresh engine has been found and put on the stranded train, the hard-pressed engine con-troller must still get the defective machine attended to and the work of the replacement engine covered. A derailment may mean anything from total rerouting or bridging a blocked line with a bus service to the intro-duction of single line working: working over one line the traffic of two, with its complex safety regulations covering speed, clamping points and providing a competent pilotman to accompany each train.

Much of what happens in the railway operating situation goes on be-hind the scenes. The men 'on call' for an emergency only appear when it happens, the railway police are quite unobtrusive until trouble flares up and the restaurant car supplies slip quietly onto the trains in their wicker hampers. Breakdown cranes, the most obvious of the emergency appliances, seem to lead an idle life but, when turned out, do miracles of lifting, jacking, packing and cajoling until a derailed locomotive is back on the rails. In parallel with all this is a commercial and administrative network of staff to sell tickets and space, others to plan trains and time-tables, some to roster, appoint and pay men, and others still to plan an en-gineer's 'possession' or the locomotive 'shopping' programme; in all a total, complex but fascinating activity.

6 Travel for Pleasure

Probably the most obvious railway hobby is that of travelling for its own sake. This can be as simple and cheap as taking advantage of a bargain fare opportunity to travel over some of the many types of interesting branch line or as luxurious as travelling from London to Scotland on one of the overnight sleeper services. There is a real sense of self indulgence in joining such a train at King's Cross after the evening commuters have gone home and been replaced by long distance passengers and the bustle of parcels and mail loadings. The feeling increases as the train races through former junctions at Sandy, Huntingdon and Holme and a good dinner is followed by coffee, then the process of settling down in the comfortable sleeping compartment to allow the reassuring sounds of the train to bring the bounty of sleep. A morning cup of tea and an unhurried gaze at the North Sea off Carnoustie is a good preparation for a day's business or pleasure in Aberdeen before, perhaps, repeating the process by travelling north to Inverness and then back to London via the West Coast route.

BR does a great deal to cater for the enjoyment of rail travel and its various travel and enquiry offices are worth visiting. They will provide literature not only on bargain fares and on such facilities as the sleeper, shipping, motorail and packaged holiday services but also on individual places worth visiting. A leaflet describes the various 'Awaydays', others give train services for individual routes, and there are special brochures such as that entitled 'Walks in the Peak National Park' which lists seven walks to be enjoyed by using stations on the Manchester – Sheffield Hope Valley line. To the pleasure of the journey can also be added a worthwhile railway objective such as a walk along the quay at Lowestoft, Weymouth or Dover or a look at the passing shipping from Craigendoran or Harwich town, a few hours amid the bustle at Leeds or York, or watching the working of the suburban services at London Bridge. On all journeys a copy of the Ian Allan *Pre-Grouping Atlas* adds to the interest by helping to identify the remaining traces of routes and junctions of the past. Those travelling to and from Europe will derive valuable help from Cook's Continental Timetable and from such societies as the Continental Railway Circle. Assistance is also available from the London offices of foreign railways and tourist agencies, from travel agents and, frequently, from railway societies in the destination country.

The BR system still comprises some 11,000 route miles, all of it interesting but some of it especially worth seeing. Some routes have special features of scenic or other significance that make them outstanding and the mention of a few less obvious examples will serve to demonstrate the wealth of interest available, often where it might be least expected. Thus the observant passenger on the Cornish branch line from Liskeard to Looe will spot the remains of the canal whose route this line usurped while the beautiful branch from Llandudno to Blaenau Ffestiniog not only provides a good example of the ingenuity of railway builders in following valleys and contours but also has an almost theatrical climax when it bursts from the final tunnel upon the slate mountains that dominate its terminus.

Euston – Glasgow: a classic run

Most of the main lines are a 'must' but especially the L&NWR main line from modern Euston to Glasgow, the gateway to West Scotland. No longer can the journey be approached through the famous Doric arch in the station forecourt, but the trains still draw away from Euston up an incline once worked by a stationary engine and, as they head north, they vie with the old and new rivals represented by the Grand Union Canal and the M1 motorway. On through the Midlands and the railway town of Crewe, a stretch of the industrial North West with its canals, mills and factories gives way eventually to a sight of Morecambe Bay and possibly of one of the foreign or other preserved locomotives in steam at the former Carnforth motive power depot. Gentle arable scenery gives way in turn to majestic and beautiful hills until Shap Summit is reached and the hard climb becomes a downward rush through Penrith and then along the course of the River Petteril and into Carlisle. From here to Glasgow the Glasgow & South Western Railway trains took the easy route through Dumfries and Kilmarnock but the proud Caledonian Railway taught its enginemen to lift their heavy trains over Beattock summit before passing through Carstairs, junction for Edinburgh, and then past the steelworks at Motherwell into Glasgow itself.

To complete the experience really demands that the journey be continued over the West Highland line to Mallaig, behind a pair of locomo-

A train of varied passenger stock (the leading coach is still in the old livery) on the beautiful and wild West Highland Line near Mallaig. The marks left by lifting track can be seen beside the line

tives which pass down the north bank of the Clyde and along the shores of Loch Long and Loch Lomond before entering Rob Roy country with its tumbling waterfalls and the first sight of the mountains. After the Oban and Mallaig lines separate at Crianlarich, the latter follows a route of more mountains, lochs, viaducts and horseshoe bends, ancient strongholds and beautiful moors and passes under Britain's only snowshed, at Cruach Cutting, before skirting Loch Treig and following the valley to Fort William. The remaining stretch to Mallaig and its steamer services to the Hebridean islands is equally dramatic, exchanging the splendour of Ben Nevis for a green, lochside route interspersed with tunnels and monuments until it reaches the open waters of the Sound of Sleat.

At the other extreme, geographically and in character, is the former GWR route beyond Exeter the approach to which, curiously, used to see SR and GWR trains for the west pass in opposite directions. Vying for the traffic to Plymouth and beyond, the SR vaunted its Atlantic Coast Express – but the GWR had the attractive scenic section through Dawlish and even fitted its stock with special windows to allow the sun's ultra-violet rays to filter through and stimulate the holiday feeling. After crossing the gentle farmland of South Devon and pausing at Plymouth, the line crosses the Tamar via Brunel's magnificent Royal Albert Bridge to wind through the many faces of Cornwall, from the curves of Menheniot and the china clay area of Par and St Austell to the flatter tin mine country around Redruth and Camborne and, eventually, the port and terminus at Penzance.

The former Midland Railway has retained only the Derby – Matlock portion of its beautiful route through the gentle woods and rippling waters of the Derbyshire Dales; travelling over the same company's lonely route from Leeds to Carlisle is difficult because of the sparse train service, but both journeys are worth the effort. So too are two alternative onwards stages, either round the coast over the route of the old Furness Railway or from Carlisle to Newcastle along the course of the infant River Tyne. Continuing north from Newcastle takes the traveller along the coast of Northumbria and through the old border town of Berwick, providing the imaginative with an idea of the countryside over which border quarrels, cattle raids and local family feuds were once everyday occurrences. The Central Wales line from Swansea to Shrewsbury provides nearly four hours of superb, gentle scenery but if this is too difficult to fit into an itinerary, the line from Newport through Hereford and Ludlow will give almost as much pleasure. Again, the traveller should go on if possible, through Welshpool and the very heart of Wales to the Dovey estuary and then to Pwllheli or south to Aberystwyth.

Branch line travel

Branch lines should not be neglected. That from Wrexham to Liverpool is full of interest and contrast and the $65\frac{3}{4}$ miles from Tonbridge to Reading gives a good picture of the three southern counties it traverses. The remaining lines beyond Inverness lead to a strangely beautiful but lonely world. The route through the Stroudwater Valley from Swindon to Gloucester takes the traveller back in time to the heyday of the local woollen industry, and the branch from Par to Newquay reveals much of the Cornish china clay workings and the lines that serve them. The Eastern Region branch from Wickford out to Burnham-on-Sea and Southminster shows the calmer face of Essex, and the old East Suffolk line from Ipswich through Beccles to Lowestoft tells much of rural England and a different age.

Then, for the energetic, there is a possible marathon across the Fens and Wolds by way of March, Lincoln and New Holland Pier, where a crossing to Hull on the Humber Ferry will eventually lead to Filey and Scarborough. Nor must the Southern Region be forgotten just because it is primarily a commuter's line. The Seaford branch is just the thing for a windy day; the Lymington branch gives access to the Yarmouth ferry, and a trip out from London to Gravesend can be turned into a circular tour by crossing the ferry there and returning on the Fenchurch Street line.

The drama of industry

In the search for scenery the fascination of industry should not be overlooked. Just on the short trip from Birmingham to Wolverhampton it is possible to see a steelworks with its own wagons carrying huge slabs of slag and tipping metal scrap into the furnaces from a raised platform and with BR wagons bringing in coal and limestone. At a railhead for steel traffic near the same line steel rods are unloaded from bogie bolster wagons by electro-magnetic cranes and, not far away, oil trains feed the huge oil terminal at West Bromwich. The lawns and veteran signal at Cadbury's lineside factory at Bournville to the south contrast with the Derby and Leicester route out to Water Orton which runs past the modern Freightliner terminal and the marshalling yard at Washwood Heath, once never empty of coal trains and empties waiting to be shunted. Near the adjacent Esso oil terminal is a short stretch where rail, motorway and water routes run in parallel to be followed by a Ketton cement terminal and then the power station, waterworks and Distillers Company complex at Water Orton where the Derby and Nuneaton routes part company.

Traditional practice has been for traffic to and from railway private sidings to be moved within the private sidings by the motive power of the firm concerned. This has resulted in many miles of standard-gauge track, connected to the main line but operated by a considerable variety of locomotives and, in some cases, rolling stock. The biggest operator is still the National Coal Board despite the process of colliery closures, and this body was even operating a few steam locomotives as recently as

Contrasting industrial scene: two locomotives on a train of ballast wagons in a limestone quarry

1975, although most had been displaced by diesels or gone into reserve. The NCB also has a considerable network underground linking the coal faces with the winding shafts. To reduce fire risks the locomotives are normally of the battery electric or flameproof diesel type, and the passenger cars and coal tubs are of a narrow gauge suited to the confined space in which they operate.

The British Steel Corporation also operates extensive private sidings for moving coal, scrap, oils and acids, finished products and even, in one steelworks, torpedo-shaped wagons loaded with molten steel. Other large firms, such as the Ford Motor Company, have their own networks and there are many smaller locations e.g. coal concentration depots, which have a single locomotive. The government departments and HM Forces operate both standard-gauge and narrow-gauge lines at ordnance and storage depots while some industries, clay and sand firms, waterworks and even agricultural concerns among them, still use a narrow-gauge industrial railway as part of their production process.

Many industrial steam locomotives, displaced by rationalisation, have been kept at work by the preserved lines but other examples, such as the fireless locomotive which worked on waste steam, are now quite rare.

Even so a great deal of interest remains in this subject and items still in use range from slag wagons at the GKN works at Cardiff to Tarmac's wagon tippler at Hayes. Static preservation is exemplified by the National Trust's collection at Penrhyn Castle while the West Lancashire Light Railway at Hesketh Bank provides a good example of what can be done by a small group of enthusiasts using industrial equipment. Societies catering for interests in this sphere include the Industrial Railway Society, which produces some excellent publications on the subject, the Industrial Locomotive Society, the Narrow Gauge Railway Society and the Brockham Museum Trust.

Among the many other unusual aspects of railways are trains that follow unusual route combinations. The summer holiday services produce trains from Leicester to Skegness, Manchester to Yarmouth (via Lincoln and March) and Scarborough to Liverpool, the services on Table 51 of the BR timetable include such examples as Poole–Newcastle, Cardiff–Manchester and the Bristol–Glasgow/Edinburgh trains which divide at Carstairs, while the 15·15 from Manchester reaches its shipping connection at Parkeston Quay via Sheffield, Nottingham and Peterborough. Other boat train services provide interesting examples of luggage and passenger handling and of the way the railway operation has to be manipulated to ensure the maximum use of expensive vessels.

A visit to a station at night will also reveal much of interest and may afford the opportunity to post a letter in one of the Royal Mail vehicles in which sorting continues while the train is still in motion. Getting near a marshalling yard in the late evening may not be easy but can be very rewarding, and while a notice about Sunday engineering work may mean delay to the passenger it will spell something better for those interested in railways. The same may apply to replacing a bridge, righting a derailment or just taking a chance by going on a mystery excursion. There is always something interesting or unusual to be enjoyed.

7 Railway History

Railway history is a fascinating study which not only helps in the understanding of today's railway system but also sheds a lot of light on national history, since the evolution of the railways reflected the development of the nation. The subject also gives the opportunity for original research and the chance to make an individual contribution, either through the preservation movement or by recording the items and locations which are still disappearing in the face of continuing railway rationalisation. Apart from a broad understanding of the evolutionary pattern of the industry, some knowledge of the sources of further information and a taste for the variety and fascination of the past, it requires little else save imagination and accuracy.

Following the success of the Stockton & Darlington and Liverpool & Manchester schemes came the first trunk lines, from London to Birmingham and Bristol. More and more lines were then promoted to produce the years of the 'Railway Mania' with thousands of speculators looking for quick profits, every town wanting a railway and every railway determined to be a trunk route. The era produced such legendary financial manipulators as George Hudson, labelled 'The Railway King', engineers like Isambard Kingdom Brunel and many other colourful men of vision and enterprise. It was also a time of intense rivalry starting from the moment a new company was formed, to threaten the business or arouse the expansionist instincts of an existing line, continuing with a Parliamentary battle for the legislation that each company needed as its authority for acquiring land, and usually finishing with one line ruining, leasing or merging with the other. In this way most of the eventual main lines emerged, a good example being the London & North Western Railway which was formed in 1846 from the London & Birmingham, Grand Junction and Manchester & Birmingham Railways.

The second half of the nineteenth century brought not only the rise of the main companies, each with its own distinctive features ranging from locomotive livery to operating practice, but also a round of legislation giving rates protection to the hard hit canals, improving safety standards and laying down stipulations covering minimum service standards and things like special early morning fares for workmen. Apart from the Great Central Railway's London Extension, opened in 1899, all the main systems were largely complete by the advent of the racing years between 1888 and 1895 when the 541 miles of the West Coast route to Aberdeen was covered in 512 minutes and the 523½ miles of the East Coast route in 518 minutes. With all the obvious and essential routes built there was a demand for legislation allowing lower standards, and thus costs, for lines to serve rural areas. The result was the Light Railways Act of 1896 under the authority of which some of the most fascinating and individualistic of local railways were built.

The 'big four'

World War I brought government control of the 123 separate railway companies and revealed so much to be gained in terms of standardisation and co-operation that the 1921 Railways Act followed and required the grouping of all but the smallest of systems into four main networks. The new railways which came into being in 1923 comprised:

London, Midland & Scottish Railway – formed from the London & North Western Railway, Midland Railway, Lancashire & Yorkshire Railway, Caledonian Railway, Furness Railway, Glasgow & South Western Railway, Highland Railway, North London Railway, London, Tilbury & Southend Railway and various smaller systems.

London & North Eastern Railway – formed from the Great Northern Railway, Great Eastern Railway, Great Central Railway, North Eastern Railway, North British Railway, Great North of Scotland Railway, Hull & Barnsley Railway and various minor lines.

Southern Railway – formed from the South Eastern & Chatham Railway (a working union of the South Eastern and London, Chatham & Dover Railways), London, Brighton & South Coast Railway and London & South Western Railway, plus the Isle of Wight lines and others.

Great Western Railway – formed from the former Great Western Railway, Cambrian Railways, the Cardiff Railway and other South Wales lines including the Taff Vale Railway, Midland & SW Junction system and various other railways.

By the end of the 1920s road competition, started by lorries and men released when the war ended, was hitting the railways. Protective legislation was passed in 1930 and 1933 and the main line companies

A fragment of history: the Plymouth portion of the 'Atlantic Coast Express', passing Meldon Junction

improved their facilities to meet the challenge. To the Southern Railway electrification which had started in 1925, the GWR's pioneer air service (Cardiff – Torquay – Plymouth) and the 1928 introduction of non-stop runs between London and Edinburgh were added the LNER stream-lined Silver Jubilee services of 1935, with the LMS also achieving 100mph two years later. But none of this could keep the young road transport industry at bay and the railways passed into governmental con-trol with the advent of World War II low on dividends, short of capital and promoting campaigns for public sympathy.

Following the end of hostilities came the 1947 Transport Act and the nationalisation of the railways under the control of the British Transport Commission which set about repairing the ravages of the war. The Mod-ernisation Plan of 1955 followed and led to major new policies such as the decision to adopt 25kV ac electrification for the main line of the new London Midland Region and the building of a new series of steam loco-motives. By 1960 the decision to abandon steam had been taken and this was followed by the 1963 'Beeching Plan', which declared the need to concentrate on viable routes and activities and led to a new, slimmed-down railway system providing fast Inter-City trains headed by diesel locomotives, using diesel multiple units on its remaining secondary routes and using Freightliner trains and block train loads as its main form of freight activity.

Many good books have been written covering the history of each of the major railway companies and others, such as the David & Charles Regional History series, cater for those interested in particular geographical areas. Various minor railways have been covered, especially by such publishers as Oakwood Press, while other books cater for the special study of locomotive engineers, carriages, heraldry and a whole range of other aspects of railway history and development. Even so there is still ample scope for original research among the official railway records, Parliamentary material, record office and library documents and even old magazines and newspapers. Among the recommended reading list at the end of this book is a booklet which gives information on the principal sources of original material dealing with railway history.

Relics of the past

Much evidence of the past still remains visible. Within the existing railway system there are still many items and practices which provide a commentary on the past, but these are steadily getting fewer and the time to enjoy seeking them out and recording them is now. A recent case has been the closure of the line from Tuffley Junction to Gloucester Eastgate which has thrown one more elevated signal box out of work. Fortunately many pre-grouping signal boxes are still in use to enable the amateur historian to note the difference between the spacious Great Western boxes and the cosy Midland cabins, or between the functional boxes on the GN main line and the loftiness of Stockport No 2.

Semaphore signal arms have largely been standardised but decorative finials on top of signal posts frequently testify to the original parentage of the line concerned while ground signals of the disc type, called 'Dods', 'Dollies' or 'Dummies' depending on the area concerned, still preserve slight differences, as do calling-on arms, shunt signals, warning boards and many other lineside features. Crossing gates, too, repay study. To see a pair of hand–wound gates and then imagine Lincoln Central station before it lost much of its traffic is to get a glimpse of hectic railway working as it was not so many years ago.

The private stations and waiting rooms, once a perquisite of the

What on earth . . ? Put to a different use by the local authorities, this used to be the locomotive lifting sheerlegs of the Weston, Clevedon & Portishead Railway – typical of the items of railway history awaiting discovery by the observant

landowners who had to be wooed to allow the railway through their land, have disappeared but Ponsbourne Tunnel on the Hertford line remains as an example of another type of condition attached to not opposing a railway Bill. Not far away the portals of Audley End Tunnel bear the arms of Lord Braybrook, and many other structures bear heraldic or similar devices, the bridge at Runcorn among them. Historic buildings and buildings testifying to parts of the railways' past which have now disappeared are still quite commonplace. They range in func-

Another find. This unattractive old shed, found by the river at Southwold, used to be a coach on that quaint and highly individual rural railway

tion from the York headquarters of the North Eastern Railway to the great goods shed at Manchester Ardwick; in size from the castellated arch over the railway as it passes Conway Castle to the seats on Purfleet station which still bear the initials LT & S; and in function from signs and notices to the old hand crane still standing in the yard at New Mills. Although most of the smaller paraphernalia of historic significance is now in the museums a few examples of very beautiful cutlery can still be found, including a display of such items in the British Transport hotel at Newcastle. Water tanks and wagon gauges are still to be seen, along with hand barrows and even the traditional GWR boundary posts comprising an inscribed iron circle mounted on a section of old rail.

Moving further away from today's operating railway reveals even more remnants of history. A former branch line runs outside George Stephenson's old home at Wylam while far away, at Plymouth, it is still possible to trace a tunnel and other features of the route of the erstwhile Lee Moor Tramway. Tramway remains, including stone blocks, are still quite easy to find on Dartmoor, in north Wales and in the Forest of Dean, and the course of colliery lines in south Wales and the North East can still be traced given a willingness to do a little preliminary research, carry the right ordnance survey map and abandon the car in favour of walking boots when it has brought you to the area to be explored.

Developing a keen eye and being willing to tramp along long abandoned routes can produce such interesting finds as a piece of rail from the Bideford, Westward Ho & Appledore Railway put to work as part of a cattle grid, another piece of edge rail from one of the old Forest of Dean tramways, the Bagworth winding house and incline of the Leicester & Swannington Railway, any one of the swing bridge sites among Norfolk's waterways, the world's oldest metal railway bridge at Robertstown and literally hundreds of other similar finds that add not only a tremendous satisfaction to the outing but give a greater understanding of the whole course of railway history.

Whether it is one of these 'finds' buried in bracken or in a scrapyard or a piece of old railway working equipment restored and on display, railway history, like all history, is the better for a little imagination. With this the remains of a steamer paddle box at Wemyss Bay can conjure up

This old Welsh Highland Railway bridge near Beddgelert has been used to 'point' to the disused section of trackbed on the far side, which might otherwise have seemed just an ordinary woodland path

the days of the rival train services from Glasgow to the coast and the hair-raising tactics of their companion steamer services anxious to snatch passengers from one another's routes.

With imagination two old buildings near Fenchurch Street and Starcross bring back to life the cable working of the London & Blackwall Railway and the atmospheric system first used by the South Devon Railway. The same imagination can turn the overgrown tips and ridged quarry faces seen from the Llanberis Lake Railway into the living slate quarrying community in which the leader on each face was a caretaker of moral as well as of working standards, and where the discussion of religion and philosophy created a university of the open air of which the railway incline and the Padarn Railway's route down to the coast were as essential a part as railway history has always been of that of its surroundings.

8 Collecting,
Models and Modelling

A popular pastime closely connected with travelling is that of timing and recording train performance. Arch exponent of this activity was the late Cecil J. Allen, who brought to life by his descriptive accounts in the *Railway Magazine* the days when no two locomotives steamed alike and train loads and weather conditions could combine to produce either superlative or mediocre performances. Although today locomotive characteristics are more stable and the total number of trains operated is fewer, speeds are faster, connections tighter and rails get just as greasy in wet weather. Add in the complications of splitting trains, adding or unloading mail vehicles and reversing or changing engines and the recording and logging of train performance can still be a most interesting subject.

Essential equipment for the timing enthusiast is a record book or pad, an ordinary watch and a stop watch. Distances and timing points on a particular route can usually be taken from previous logs recorded in the *Railway Magazine* and the scheduled time of the train may be obtained from the same source, a railwayman or timing friend or from an unwanted working timetable. These three pieces of information are recorded before the journey starts with the running record showing actual times, speeds and remarks about traffic, weather and other conditions. For this purpose the ordinary watch is synchronised with railway time and the stop watch used for timing the interval between mileposts to give a train speed figure. Gradients are also worth including in the log and each run should bear details of the locomotive, the train concerned, the number of vehicles and the date. As more and more records are built up the interest of comparison is supplemented by a 'feel' for each run and route and eventually by a real sense of excitement as an exceptional performance is encountered and captured. The records are then stored, mulled over or discussed with others interested in the same subject and this hobby becomes as addictive as most other railway pastimes.

A railway stamp collection

Like other forms of collecting, collecting railway items has all the fun of

Hardly the prettiest sight: but under this mountain of scrap at Naval Row stands a battery electric locomotive

the chase, the interest of studying and identifying 'finds', the sense of satisfaction from securing a bargain and the enjoyable chore of mounting and displaying the results. One form of collecting that has enjoyed a new lease of life as a result of the preservation movement concerns railway letter stamps. Several of the preserved lines have revived the once common main line practice of accepting letters for rail conveyance and postage at destination, subject to the payment of an additional fee represented by a special stamp affixed to the letter to verify that the fee for conveyance had been paid. Not so many years ago all railway parcels bore special stamps to the value of the carriage charges paid; but these are now very rare, as are the colourful luggage labels once available to passengers travelling on certain crack expresses. However, ordinary luggage and parcels labels are still plentiful and can be purchased for a few pence from the stalls at exhibitions and open days.

There is a wide range of postage stamps depicting railway subjects, partly because some foreign post offices have agreements with their state railways for the carriage of parcels on their behalf. Railway centenaries have frequently been marked by the issue of a set of commemorative stamps, and both Germany and Belgium did just this in 1935 with a series showing modernisation scenes. The Belgians have also produced several other series with railway illustrations, one showing various types of railway activity and another depicting a different historical locomotive for each face value. Czechoslovakia produced a similar series, although Eastern bloc countries have tended to go more for colour than for draughtsmanship in their railway stamps. This is also true of those small states such as Monaco and San Marino, which derive a handsome

A Wickham trolley, certainly not as glamorous as the Flying Scotsman – but replete with value for the railway historian, modeller or restorer

Railway stamps from around the world – Belgium, Germany, Denmark, France, Hungary, the United States, the Soviet Union, and Honduras

income from producing postage stamps aimed more at the collector than the letter writer. New World stamps, especially those of South and Central America, have frequently featured the traditional New World locomotive with its cow catcher and its huge, spark-arresting smokestack. US issues have commemorated major railway events, such as marking the 75th anniversary of the completion of the first transcontinental railroad, and have covered various general subjects like 'honoring railroad engineers'.

Norway and Australia produced stamps to celebrate their railway centenaries in 1954, and East Germany commemorated '125 Years of German Railways' some time before the GPO produced a series of railway postage stamps in this country. However, to celebrate 150 years of British passenger railways a set of four stamps has been issued depicting Stephenson's locomotive for the Stockton & Darlington Railway, Drummond's NBR Waverley class, a 1923 GWR Castle and the locomotive unit of the new High Speed Train. Several preservation bodies produced their own commemorative covers to mark the event and included their own railway stamps to make not only an attractive collector's item but also a good investment. First day covers of this sort are best stored in a protective transparent wallet, but ordinary postage stamps depicting railway subjects are well catered for by the range of albums, books and other items marketed for the conventional stamp collector. An album, stamp hinges for mounting, a catalogue and magnifying glass to facilitate identification and tweezers for handling are, in fact, all that the collector needs to start browsing in stamp shops or negotiating with other ardent, or even lapsed, collectors.

Wide range of tickets

Collecting railway tickets is a major enthusiast pastime. The earliest tickets were hand-written paper vouchers, although tokens and cards were used by directors and other privileged travellers. The need for a simpler and more efficient system was met by Thomas Edmonson, a clerk on the Newcastle & Carlisle Railway, who devised in 1837 a booking process based on the use of a thin card ticket of $1\frac{3}{16}$ in by $2\frac{1}{4}$in which bore the journey details on the front and the date on the reverse. For many years railways used this Edmonson system which provided for the tickets to be stored in a multiple-tube rack, from which they were withdrawn in sequence for dating in a small machine prior to issue. In recent years ticket issuing has been mechanised, using machines which print the journey details onto a blank card, while more recently still a larger form of paper ticket has come back into use.

Although the early and rare tickets are now mostly lodged in museums and private collections, there is still considerable scope for the collector.

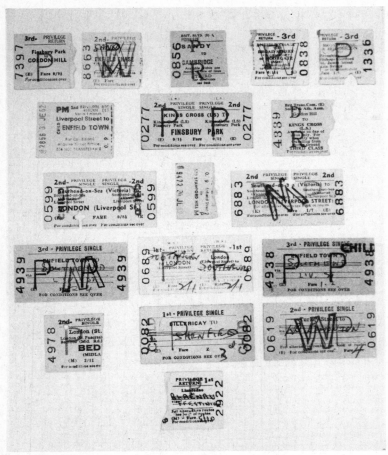

A selection of railway employees' 'privilege' tickets – 1st, 2nd, and 3rd class

The normal range of current BR tickets is extended by platform tickets, excess fare vouchers, season tickets and the like and it is still possible to find stations or travel agents issuing Edmonson tickets and other unusual items like platform tickets still showing the old currency or tickets to a range of destinations, some of which may have been closed. Other types of ticket currently available include those issued for exhibitions or other special occasions, such as the return of Sir Francis Chichester after his first historic voyage, the recently reintroduced platform ticket for Llanfairpwllgwyngyll–gogerychwyrndrob–wyllllantysilio–gogogoch, and the tickets of the various preserved lines.

A fair number of Irish tickets and pre-nationalisation BR and 'Big Four' company stocks are still circulating to extend the scope and give the collector the pleasure of rumaging through a box of tickets on an open day stall and finding a wartime Forces 'furlough' issue – or an LNER pram ticket with its small portion intended to be detached and tied to the pram when it was placed in the guard's care.

Mounting and displaying tickets

A satisfactory way of presenting a ticket collection is to use transparent corner mounts with separate mounting sheets or album pages for each group of tickets. What is difficult is to decide what the groupings shall be, for although individual companies and types of ticket make fairly obvious groupings, the same type of ticket from the same company may vary in design from series to series. The process is further complicated by the former railway practice of removing 'snips' from a ticket to reduce a full fare ticket to a child's issue, of cutting tickets diagonally and of making two singles out of one return. A specialist collector may also try to acquire tickets carrying the various types of validation punch marks or those from one particular company or line. Yet another set of variations comes from extending the hobby to include the tickets of foreign railways. All these permutations add greatly to the fascination of this particular railway hobby and the dilemma of how to present the collection can always be resolved by grouping the main railways and ticket types together and having a separate display of the items which the collector is making his speciality.

Labels, handbills and posters

The same sort of scope exists for collectors of other small railway items. Wagon labels are fascinating but fairly rare and the small handbills, which railways once produced in their thousands, tend to have been pasted up into collections or become yellow and frayed with age. Posters and former compartment pictures can still be purchased, together with signal box and other layout diagrams. Additionally, railway instructional books which were once carefully kept from the general public have now become fairly freely available as a result of British Railways realising the interest in and value of such items and, as a result, offering them for sale at Open Days and through the Collectors' Corner facility at Cardington Street, Euston and at Carnforth.

Your own railway museum

The change in BR policy has also made it possible for the enthusiast to acquire much larger relics and even to establish his own small museum. Steam engine nameplates, once given away to local authorities, football clubs and others, have become very rare and valuable but items such as signal arms can still be purchased for as little as £5–10 and the more common types of enamel sign for even less. The choice ranges from lamps to station seats, but signal equipment makes a particularly good choice. A brass 'repeater' instrument polished up, or a restored GNR

Simple but dignified, this chair will have seen some railway history since it first entered service with the Bristol & Exeter Railway

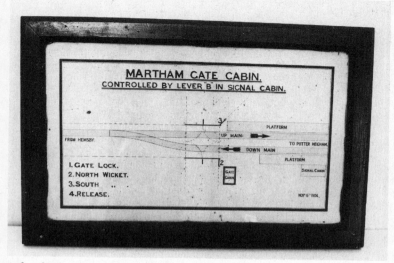

Before the electronic age: this diagram from the former Gate Cabin at Martham in Norfolk (M & GN) refers to four levers, and is dated November 1904

signal lamp with its square lamp box and tall chimney, make good display items, as do hand lamps, lever collars, tokens and tablets. Even block instruments can still be purchased for a reasonable sum to make a good centrepiece for a small, private exhibition of signalling equipment. As with other forms of collecting, much of the pleasure lies in searching out items, restoring them and then putting them on display. For those who do not have too much room the collection can be devoted to smaller items such as cap badges, uniform buttons and pay tokens, all of which can be obtained through the Collectors' Corner locations, from preservation society stalls, from dealers advertising in the railway press and by exchange or trade using journals like the Railway Collectors Newsletter.

The range of railway hobbies is enormous. Not only does it extend from train spotting to the most complicated research into, say, railway heraldry but the former could be either simple number capturing or the collection of data in order to reconstruct a locomotive's working diagram. The latter could vary from just reading a book on the subject to actually painting coats of arms, using paints to the original specification. In addition to the filming and modelling mentioned later, those with talent can derive much satisfaction from painting and drawing railway

This collection of signalling relics includes two single line key tokens, a 'repeater' instrument, a GWR hand lamp and a GNR signal lamp

subjects. Even for those without special talent it is surprising what results can be achieved with either a soft lead pencil or a black fibre-tip pen.

Records, books and films form a part of the railway hobby that allows the enthusiast to enjoy things he might not otherwise have access to and to do this at his leisure. Some excellent records of rare and evocative railway sounds have been produced by Argo Records and others and a number of firms have produced exceptionally good 8mm and 16mm films on steam, preservation and foreign railway subjects. The major booksellers have available works on all the principal railways and railway activities from David & Charles, Ian Allan and other major publishers, while firms like Oakwood Press and others have produced smaller works dealing with the smaller companies and the many bye-ways of the vast subject of railways. One area often neglected is that of the specialist secondhand and antiquarian booksellers like P. H. Edwards of Hyde and Norman Kerr of Cartmel, Lancs. The catalogue of the former includes such rare and interesting items as a booklet called *Engines at War* and the 1909 *Boys Book of Railways*, while the latter provides a 'search and offer' service to meet clients' needs from his collection of over 20,000 items and also maintains a register of collectors' special requirements.

The delight of railway hobbies is that their variety is infinite and that they can cost as little or as much in time and money as the enthusiast wishes to spend. In addition to the individual pursuits there are many pre-packaged activities, not the least being the railtours organised by a number of specialist societies and advertised in the railway magazines. Local societies provide a good forum for discussion, films and talks and several august bodies operate on a national basis, catering either for particular interests (narrow-gauge, industrial railways and individual companies) or for general interests on a very responsible plane, as with the Railway & Canal Historical Society, the Stephenson Locomotive Society, the Railway Correspondence & Travel Society, and others.

Models and Modelling

Model locomotives were being used as the presentation samples of cast iron salesmen well before the middle of the last century with the first working toys, crudely fashioned in brass, following soon afterwards. Between 1900 and the outbreak of war in 1914 the mass production of

When manners mattered: a beautifully-phrased warning notice, courtesy of GW & M. Nowadays all you would get would be DANGER – KEEP OUT – TRESPASSERS WILL BE PROSECUTED

model railways became big business with three German firms and the British company Bassett-Lowke dominating the market. Bassett-Lowke's 30,000 locomotives a year were, of course, all clockwork in the pioneer 'O' gauge of 7mm to 1ft. After the war Meccano Limited came to the fore with a basic train set costing 30 shillings, a large selection of locomotives and rolling stock and a national distribution network. Bassett-Lowke introduced the 'OO' gauge of 4mm to 1ft when they brought out the Trix Twin trains and then came the Hornby Dublo range in the same scale and available in both clockwork and 12 volt dc electric versions.

Much had changed by the time modelling reached its centenary. Smaller houses brought a demand for smaller modelling scales and the desire for greater realism brought improvements in the relationship between gauge and scale. As the main line railways have become more functional there has been an increasing interest in the detail of operation and in creating layouts with a strong historical theme. Manufacturers have responded to both these trends and there is now available not only a wide range of trains and track in packaged sets but also every conceivable individual and ancillary item. With a wheel and motor unit as a

The Peco Modelrama at Beer, Devon, is an exhibition designed to help railway modellers by showing what can be done in varying amounts of space

starting point, today's modeller can also build his own locomotive from scratch using the extensive selection of proprietory tools, materials and paints available. More modelling time and attention now goes into layout and scenery, while at the other extreme more locomotive engineers are building their own machines capable of hauling a trainload of youngsters round an outdoor track.

Broadly the modelling activity can be divided into four types, the purchase and operation of mass produced trains, track and equipment, the use of such layouts as much for the pleasure of modelling additional features as for the railway itself, the activity which builds almost everything from scratch, and the outdoor work in which the activity is more of an engineering than a modelling one. This latter area is quite distinct but also very challenging and rewarding. It is as well to start with a simple locomotive, possibly as a joint venture, and a lathe, a workshop and some money to spare are all essentials. Given good plans and a fair amount of engineering skill, aptitude and patience, the end product could be a rewarding $3\frac{1}{2}$, 5 or $7\frac{1}{4}$in-gauge locomotive or even a full scale railway laid out as part of the back garden. Newcomers to this field would be well advised to join one of the many excellent model engineering societies whose facilities cover advice, tools, test tracks and even locomotive exchange outings.

Indoor railways

Indoor modelling offers such a variety of scales, manufacturers and other options that it is important to take careful decisions before making a start, since the failure to do so inevitably brings either an unnecessary conversion cost or vain regrets over not having chosen differently. The decisions to make cover how much space can be allocated to the layout, whether it is to have a main line theme, a passenger theme, a foreign theme or be a mixed activity and whether the emphasis is to be on running or modelling. One's aptitude for modelling, wiring and designing scenery should also be considered. Other steps worth taking before starting the spending process are a visit to the local railway exhibition, the purchase of the principal manufacturers' catalogues and a chat with the local model shop proprietor. The exhibition visit will be especially valuable since it will not only show what can be achieved in a given space but also provide details of local societies and model shops in the neighbourhood.

The various scales and gauges available to the indoor modeller using proprietory items comprise:

N	1 : 148 or 1 : 160 scale	9mm gauge
OOO	2mm : 1ft scale	9·5mm gauge
TT3	3mm : 1ft scale	12mm gauge
HO	3·5mm : 1ft scale	16·5mm gauge
OO	4mm : 1ft scale	16·5mm gauge
EM	4mm : 1ft scale	18mm gauge
S	3/16th in : 1ft scale	$\frac{7}{8}$in gauge
O	7mm : 1ft scale	32mm gauge

The original 'O' gauge is now largely the preserve of the collector or extreme devotee because of the room it takes up. It was supplanted by 'OO' which has remained the most popular gauge partly because of the very wide range of commercial items available. The 18mm gauge of 'EM' gives a truer relationship between scale and gauge but the range of components stocked by the model shops is lower and so more hand building is necessary. The 'S' scale is even more the sphere of the model builder and for very intricate modelling, making maximum use of a small space; 'OOO' or 'Two Millimetre' represents a challenging and rewarding medium. The range of proprietory items in 'N' gauge is good and this is very popular for achieving a lot of variety in a limited amount of room, while 'TT3' provides a popular intermediate position between 'N' and 'OO'.

Specialist modelling societies cater for many of these gauges, including the EM Gauge Society, the Gauge 'O' Guild, the Three Millimetre Society and the 2mm Scale Association. All exist to help modellers in the medium concerned and some operate a components service. Model railway clubs exist in most towns and have an area association to co-ordinate their activities. Other societies cater for such special interests as the exchange of information among Hornby train collectors, for those interested in North American railroads and for linking users of international scales.

Having chosen the gauge and scale combination best suited to your interests, space and pocket, you will then need to devise your operational layout. Manufacturers' catalogues will provide details of track dimensions, radii and sample layouts. Booklets are also available on this sub-

Faithful reconstruction in miniature: the Dart Valley's Staverton Bridge, handbuilt in 2mm scale using thin card and commercially-produced 'brick' paper

ject. When the decision has been made the main track and principal junctions can then be laid on the foundation board using proprietory 'ballast' strips. Make sure to leave adequate room for stations, locomotive and goods depots, sidings, scenery and, particularly, for extensions and access. It is wise to buy new track, a good principal locomotive and other basic items, but as your layout develops you can use secondhand equipment and stock to create the atmosphere of a period working railway rather than one that has just emerged from the manufacturer's packing.

Except for vintage clockwork models, trains are normally powered by domestic electricity using a transformer to step it down to 12 volts DC. From the transformer a lead passes to each rail so that the current for the small motor inside the body of the locomotive is picked up through the wheels from one rail and returned to complete the circuit via the other. Points are so designed that in addition to changing the route they also isolate the current from one route and allow it to flow in the direction for which they are set. In the more sophisticated systems points can be changed by small electric motors working from a console equivalent of a signal box. Signals too can be electrically worked and linked to the operation of the route with which they are associated. Room must be allowed when planning the layout both for the operating panel and for getting at wiring or other faults.

Miniature scenery

Making scenery and other items for a model railway layout can be as much fun as actually operating it. Model figures, sheets of 'stonework' paper and packets of 'grass' are probably best purchased but making tunnels and other structures from a wooden framework and papier maché is both rewarding and demanding, not only in the final touches of realism but also in ensuring clearance for the frame of the locomotive as it swings round a curve and allowing for access in the case of a derailment. A sure sign of a keen modeller is his propensity for collecting almost any small item or piece of material and then using it to good purpose in his layout. Small logos from advertisements in colour magazines become lineside hoardings in this way and the matches of even the most inveterate smoker can be used when there is some fencing to be provided.

Drawing up timetables

However satisfying modelling may be, operating the trains is a pastime in which the pleasure increases with the complexity until a situation is reached in which the model layout produces most of the operating features of the full size railway. Timetables can be compiled, too, by timing each operation with a stopwatch and then establishing a basis on which

This Dartmoor railway scene at the Pendon Museum of Miniature Landscape & Transport will repay detailed study, from the construction of the Brunel trestle viaduct to the tiny figures and luggage inside the train

to scale up the time dimension of the activity in line with the size dimension. Having established running times for branch line trains and for fast and slow trains on the main line, freight trains can be added to the list and times worked out for their shunting work at goods yards and sidings.

After assessing each operation and creating a timetable, operating the model railway to it not only creates an added dimension to the hobby but gives a useful insight into the sort of problems that arise in the real life situation. A compromise will have to be made, for example, between keeping the branch line train fully occupied and stopping so many main line trains to connect with it that the whole of the main line operation is disrupted. One solution is to use the branch train for occasional main line journeys, another is to take the engine away for some freight work, while yet a third is to use a railcar or railbus to reduce the branch line costs, all alternatives which would be considered by any working railwayman engaged in train planning. Further operational fun comes from planning for engineering work and other special events, and if you keep a diary or controller's log recording these incidents and developments it will provide excellent reading when your mood is reflective rather than active.

Modelling reference

To assist the railway modeller there are some good magazines devoted to the hobby including the *Model Railway Constructor, Railway Modeller* and the two MAP journals, *Model Railways* and *Meccano Magazine*. This firm also produces useful booklets and engineering publications while the Peco people, in addition to their model railway products, have put together an interesting and useful exhibition at the Peco Modelrama at Beer in Devon. Here layouts have been set up to show just how they could fit into a hall, loft or shed, or even just a shelf space. There are also photographs, a workshop, relics, gardens and refreshments as well as the passenger-carrying Beer Heights Light Railway. Another location that the modeller should really try to visit is the Pendon Museum of Miniature Landscape & Transport at Long Wittenham where railway and countryside scenes of the 1930s have been recreated with incredible care and accuracy and where John Ahern's pioneer layout is also on display. Another special facility for the modeller is the recent availability, through a joint venture between BR's Western Region and the Oxford Publishing Company, of copies of thousands of official railway engineering drawings covering not only locomotives, stock and other items, but also going back to broad-gauge days.

The variety of interest for the modeller is endless. In addition to planning, building and working his layout he can photograph it, write about it and display it. The interest will take him out to places like Pendon and Beer, and to museums with models, to rallies and exhibitions, to model and secondhand shops and to the local club or society for a chat about his own layout and experiences and the pleasure of hearing about those of fellow enthusiasts. He will also watch the main line railway with eyes for new ideas to incorporate in his miniature replica of it.

9 Railway Photography

The main difference between photographing railway subjects and other forms of photography lies more in the variety of subjects and conditions and in the techniques of location and composition than in the photographer's equipment. As in other fields, the better the equipment the better the end result is likely to be but, because the subjects are so varied, the most modest of cameras can produce satisfying pictures if the user takes some care over what he is doing and understands the rudiments of the photographic art.

As explained in *Good Photography Made Easy* (also in this series), photography is all about light. The amount of light passing through a camera lens depends on how wide it is open – and these *aperture settings* are given an 'f' code in which f11 is a wider aperture than f16 and so on. How long it is open for – is determined by the *shutter speed*. Thus a wide aperture and a slow shutter speed lets in the maximum light; a narrow aperture and a fast shutter speed restricts the light. Choosing which to use is determined partly by the light available, partly by the need to use a fast shutter speed to avoid blurring moving objects and partly by the fact that the larger the aperture, the smaller the *depth of field* or the distance in clear focus. The other principal variable is the sensitivity, or speed, of the film. The slower the film – the lower its ASA or DIN rating – the longer light must be allowed through the camera lens.

Cameras vary from the cheaper, fixed speed camera where the aperture can be varied only for bright or dull conditions to the most elaborate pieces of expensive precision machinery, including technically superb plate cameras capable of the most detailed reproduction. In this range the simple camera is certainly not to be despised, but there are things it just will not do. The 'average' shutter speed setting means, for example, that it cannot take a picture of a fast-moving train because this will have changed its position perceptibly while the shutter has been open. Thus trains in motion should be photographed from an acute angle unless the photographer is setting out deliberately to produce a blurred image in order to convey a sense of speed. With a camera that has few refinements it is worth wasting some exposures to get the feel of what the camera will do, after which a thoughtful search for the right subjects will show just how effective such cameras can be.

Cine is a subject all on its own, based on the same principles as still photography but requiring extra techniques to produce continuity and in panning across or zooming into a subject, since such movements must both be even and regular and also recognise changes in light and proportion. Again, the dearer the camera the more equipment it should have to handle such technical problems, and once the potential photographer has decided what he can afford the decision about whether to take cine films depends upon whether the extra expense of processing, projectors, screens, splicing equipment and so forth is considered good value against the tremendous satisfaction of having a live record. For spectacular action events and rare moments a cine camera is unbeatable, but for other events a conventional camera can be a good and competent friend.

Choice of camera

Allowing the cine, polaroid, miniature and other camera devotees their preference still leaves the ordinary photographer with a very personal choice to make. In fact, the answer may well be two cameras. Without spending an excessive sum it is possible to purchase an excellent combination of a good 35mm single lens reflex model and an automatic half-frame camera, both with built in light meters. The former is small enough to be versatile, has a good range of aperture and shutter speed settings, can be used with alternative lenses and shows in the viewfinder the image which appears through the lens. The latter only has to be pointed and the shutter release pressed and, with reasonable care in the pointing, the good quality lens and automatically adjusting shutter will produce lots of good quality pictures. Together, the two give the photographer the choice of black and white or colour and of careful, quality pictures or quick, effective event recording.

Like cameras, films are also a matter of individual preference. The slower the film, the less grain and thus the bigger the clear enlargements that can be made from it. Slow films also give better contrast between light and shadow and while a fast film will do wonders when the light is poor it tends to produce flat and dull negatives in ordinary light. For black and white pictures 125 ASA is a good, average speed with the general rule being to use slower films in the south and faster ones in the north. Colour films, which can be either of the negative or transparency type, are slower. Supplementary camera equipment is not essential although a lenshood, lens brush, a yellow filter for sharpening cloud images and a notebook in which to record the exposures are all useful.

Choice of subject will depend on the photographer's interests but an infinite variety is available. Locomotives and trains alone could fulfill all the challenge a railway photographer needs and many suitable locations have been detailed earlier in the book. It is worthwhile trying something different at the popular locations and while an 'against-the-light' shot as a train thunders over a bridge overhead may often have a disappointing outcome, it could just produce the picture of a lifetime. Trains departing, trains watched, trains early in the day or season are all capable of producing that extra bit of satisfaction; and if the filming has to take place in the height of the season, have the patience to wait until the locomotive fire is being raked out or you can catch the driver wondering how he will ever move his load the way the engine has been steaming lately.

Locations and scenery

Main line railways offer tremendous scope for train photography. Although diesel locomotives may not be as interesting as their steam counterparts they work such a variety of services in such a variety of locations as to make up for this. Again patience and ingenuity are as important as equipment and skills. To catch a train at Bournville when a boat is passing on the adjacent canal takes some doing, while at Dawlish the angriest waves always seem determined to display their pictorial splendour either just before or just after the passage of a train. Usually train photographs need at least one other railway feature included, although care should be taken to avoid clutter. The point is made in the photograph of a train at Shap where the signal box nameboard makes it clear that this is the famous summit and not just one more lonely stretch of railway; and thus the picture immediately becomes evocative.

Other aspects of railways are equally exciting. Station architecture offers examples from the twin towers of Bury St Edmunds to the empty shell of Southampton Town, and passenger equipment provides such rarities as an old watering barrow or a platform seat with iron supports cast to represent rustic woodwork. Crowd and other action shots make good material whether it be relaying or ballast cleaning work by an engineer's train, the visit of an inspection saloon or a commuter crowd bursting from a Waterloo platform. Summer excursion arrivals at Rams-

Sheringham Station on a North Norfolk Railway 'Members' Day', showing the range of older vehicles which has been preserved. There is a GN suburban set in the middle of the waiting train, and railbuses and freight stock on the other line

gate or the activity at any of the railway ports make exciting challenges too, and the railwayman taking up his locomotive or signal box duty, complete with food in his 'snap' tin, or the lookout man with warning horn to his lips are all as much a part of working railway life as the trains they deal with.

Pursuing railway history with a camera gives a double reward from the excitement of chase and discovery and the satisfaction of recording something which may soon disappear. Just walking an old branch line may turn up anything from stone blocks and early rails to a decaying slate wagon with its coupling hanging forlorn from the single central buffer. This area produces its problems, of course. The excitement of discovering an old coach may be followed by some frustration in trying to identify it and to come to the end of the Mid-Suffolk line's abortive extension beyond Laxfield raises the problem of conveying that this is not just another blackberry bush. Making interesting finds stand out sufficiently to be recorded is a whole art in itself.

Remember the question of access and rights. Private property should not be intruded upon in person or by filming, but the freedom to photograph railway subjects to which public access is available is generally accepted. This also applies to open days and similar events, but taking photographs is not usually permitted in museums. On BR a permit is required, and is only issued in certain circumstances, to photograph away from the locations to which travellers normally have access, but local officials are often very helpful where assistance is required for a special, worthwhile purpose where risk or cost is not involved and where helping in one instance is not likely to produce a flood of other requests. The copyright of a photograph is vested in the photographer, the right to allow or deny photography in the owner of the object concerned. Special care over permissions and payment is necessary where the picture is to be used for commercial purposes.

Railway photography for commercial ends is well cared for by the official BR photographers and other professionals. The only advice to be offered here is that outlets for amateur colour work are very few and that those that do exist call for transparencies, preferably 5in by 4in, and certainly not less than $2\frac{1}{4}$in square. The demand for black and white prints for reproduction is slightly higher, especially where good illustrations and a good article are presented together to a magazine.

One other area requiring thought is that of an effective storage and recording system for easy use and enjoyment. Investment in a negative storage album is important to ensure that pictures taken with much care and effort do not deteriorate. By numbering each negative on the record sheet such albums provide and giving the print the same number, retrieval is easy. This method also permits the prints to be presented in subject order, either in albums or boxes or on display cards. It is as good and as simple an idea as any to record the scene and circumstances on the back of the actual print using a label showing details of the subject and its negative number and then adding one of the small name-and-address labels that one can have printed quite cheaply. Transparencies should be placed in the special mounts available and then stored in racked boxes.

A few other points are worth making. Plenty of advice is available to the beginner from suppliers, magazines and also from photographic clubs and societies. Railway societies can help the photographer in other ways, particularly those that arrange tours and thus give the photographer access to places he might not otherwise reach. Societies, especially those concerned with Continental railways, will give advice on taking photographs abroad (where there can be hazards as well as extra scope), ranging from carrying the purchase receipt for the benefit of Customs Officers to making absolutely sure that photography is permitted before waving a camera about, especially in Eastern European states. Finally, after all these things have been thought about and the greatest care put into equipment, choice of subject, picture composition and camera technique, the real point of the whole exercise is that it should be interesting and enjoyable.

Reference

The full addresses and telephone numbers of the main operational 'light' railways are listed below but the locations are not staffed all the time; there may be difficulty in making contact by telephone, especially outside the peak periods. Letters do get attended to but it is a great help if requests are kept simple and a stamped and addressed envelope provided for the reply:

Bluebell Railway Ltd, Sheffield Park Station, Uckfield, Sussex. Tel: Newick 2370.

Dart Valley Light Railway Ltd, Buckfastleigh Station, Devon. Tel: Buckfastleigh 2338.

Fairbourne Railway Ltd, Beach Road, Fairbourne, Gwynedd. Tel: Fairbourne 362.

Festiniog Railway Company Porthmadog, Gwynedd. Tel: Portmadog 2384.

Isle of Man Railway Company, PO Box 30, Douglas, Isle of Man. Tel: Douglas 4646/7.

Keighley & Worth Valley Light Railway Ltd, Haworth Station, Keighley, West Yorkshire. Tel: Haworth 43629.

Kent & East Sussex Railway, Tenterden Town Station, Tenterden, Kent. Tel: Tenterden 2943.

Lakeside & Haverthwaite Railway Company Ltd, The Station, Haverthwaite, Ulverston, Cumbria. Tel: Newby Bridge 594.

Leighton Buzzard Narrow Gauge Railway Society Ltd, Page's Park, Billington Road, Leighton Buzzard, Beds. Tel: Leighton Buzzard 3888.

Llanberis Lake Railway, Llanberis, Gwynedd. Tel: Llanberis 549.

Manx Electric Railway, Douglas and Snaefell Mountain Railway, Laxey, Isle of Man. Write to Manx Electric Railway Board, 1 Strathallan Crescent, Douglas, Isle of Man. Tel: Douglas 4549.

Middleton Railway, Hunslet Moor, Leeds, Yorks.

North Norfolk Railway Company Ltd, Sheringham Station, Sheringham, Norfolk. Tel: Sheringham 2045.

North Yorkshire Moors Railway, Pickering Station, Park Street, Pickering, North Yorkshire. Tel: Pickering 72508.

Ravenglass & Eskdale Railway Company Ltd, Ravenglass, Cumbria. Tel: Ravenglass 226.

Romney, Hythe & Dymchurch Light Railway Company, New Romney, Kent. Tel: New Romney 2353.

Severn Valley Railway Company Ltd, Railway Station, Bewdley, Hereford & Worcs. Tel: Bewdley 403816.

Sittingbourne & Kemsley Light Railway Ltd, Sittingbourne, Kent. Tel: Sittingbourne 24899.

Snowdon Mountain Railway Ltd, Llanberis, Gwynedd. Tel: Llanberis 223.

Talyllyn Railway Company, Wharf Station, Tywyn, Gwynedd. Tel: Tywyn 710472.

Torbay Steam Railway, Queens Park Station, Paignton, Devon. Tel: Paignton 55872.

Vale of Rheidol Light Railway, British Railways, Aberystwyth, Dyfed. Tel: Aberystwyth 2377.

Welshpool & Llanfair Light Railway Preservation Company Ltd, Llanfair Caereinion, Powys. Tel: Llanfair Caereinion 441.

Details of all types of railway societies and of preservation activities are given in Avon-Anglia's *Railway & Steam Enthusiasts' Handbook* and in the ARPS Year Book. In the event of difficulty a stamped, addressed envelope should be sent to the former at 9 Poplar Avenue, Bristol BS9 2BE. Railway preservation locations are also grouped by area in the Year Book and in Avon-Anglia's smaller summary of historic transport locations entitled *Guide to Light Railways, Steamers & Historic Transport*. A few groupings, aimed at enabling the visitor to see the maximum number of locations with the least travelling, are suggested below:

Wales – Fairbourne, Festiniog, Llanberis Lake, Talyllyn, Vale of Rheidol, Welshpool & Llanfair, Great Orme, Snowdon Mountain, Bala Lake and Welsh Highland Railways, Penrhyn Castle and Corris Museums.

Scotland – Strathspey and Lochty Railways, Royal Scottish, Glasgow Transport and Scottish Railway Preservation Society (Falkirk) Museums, Glasgow Underground Railway.

South East – Bluebell, Kent & East Sussex, Romney Hythe & Dymchurch and Sittingbourne & Kemsley Railways, South Eastern Steam Centre.

South West – Dart Valley, Torbay, Bicton Woodland, Lappa Valley Railways.

South – Volks Electric, East Somerset and West Somerset Railways and Seaton Tramway, Great Western Society and Dowty collections, Dean Forest and Bristol Suburban Railway Society locations, Isle of Wight.

West Midlands – Severn Valley, Foxfield, Chasewater Park, Drayton Manor, Hilton Valley Railways, Ironbridge Gorge and two Birmingham museums.

East Midlands – Cadeby Light and Stapleford Railways, Main Line Steam Trust, Shackerstone, Dinting, Midland Railway and Leicestershire Museum of Technology locations.

East – North Norfolk, Lincolnshire Coast and Bressingham lines, Nene Valley and Stour Valley steam centres, Walton pier railway, Audley End.

Home Counties – Leighton Buzzard, Knebworth House and Whipsnade Railways, Syon Park, Quainton, Science Museum and Great Western Society collections, Pendon Museum of Miniature Landscape and Transport.

North West – Lakeside, Ravenglass & Eskdale Railways, collections at Bury, Southport, Lytham and Carnforth, Blackpool Coastal Tramway.

North East – Keighley & Worth Valley, North Yorkshire Moors, Middleton and Derwent Railways, Yorkshire Dales steam centre, National Railway Museum.

Isle of Man – Douglas Horse Tramway, Isle of Man, Manx Electric and Snaefell Mountain Railways.

BR passenger travel enquiries should normally be made to the nearest travel centre (although local stations can provide local train service information), details of which are given in telephone directories and in the front of the BR timetable. *Bus service information* for any part of the National Bus Company system can be obtained from the local NBC head office or travel centre. *London Transport* has enquiry offices at Piccadilly Circus, St James's Park, Kings Cross, Euston, Oxford Circus and Victoria stations and a telephone enquiry number (01–222 1234). Details of *LT poster and booklet sales* and of the extensive range of maps and leaflets can be obtained from the Poster Shop at St James's Park Underground station or the head office at 55 Broadway, London SW1H 0BD. There are *cheap fare facilities* on London Transport while those on BR include Awayday fares for day outings, Weekend and 17-Day Returns, Economy Returns which have to be booked three weeks in advance, Runabout Season and ordinary Season Tickets, All Line Rover Tickets covering the whole of the country and a number of other local and special occasion reductions.

Train spotting is encouraged at suitable locations on the main line system, and restrictions only operate to ensure sensible behaviour and safety and to avoid interference with the task of running the railway. Increasing train speeds make it essential for spotters to keep well away from platform edges. *Photographers* are permitted ordinary access to places regularly used by the public. Permits for other points are only issued in special circumstances, and where photographs are taken for commercial purposes a charge is made for facilities and supervision. So far as installation visits are concerned, individual applications cannot normally be entertained and party visits have to be carefully controlled for operational and security reasons. The contact in all these cases is the *Public Relations Officer* of the local Divisional office or the Regional headquarters at:

Eastern – Headquarters Offices, York YO1 1HT (0904 53022)

London Midland – Euston House, Eversholt Street, London NW1 1DF (01–387 9400)

Scottish – Buchanan House, 58 Port Dundas Road, Glasgow G4 OHG (041–332 9811)

Southern – Waterloo Station, London SE1 8SE (01–928 5151)
Western Region – Paddington Station, London W2 1HA (01–723 7000)

The main British tunnels over 2 miles long are the Severn, Totley, Woodhead, Standedge, Sodbury, Disley, Festiniog, Bramhope and Cowburn Tunnels and the principal summits those at Drumochter, Corrour, Slochd, Aisgill, Perth-Argyll boundary and Beattock, all over 1,000ft above sea level.

Train classes for operating and train description purposes are broadly as follows:

1 Express passenger, postal or 'emergency' train
2 Local passenger train
3 Express parcels train
4 Express freight train composed of vehicles capable of running at 75mph
5 Empty passenger coaches
6 Semi-express freight train, each vehicle fitted with brakes worked from the locomotive
7/8 Freight trains of a lower classification
9 Freight trains not fitted with through brakes.

For the general railway enthusiast good value is provided by the *Railway Magazine*, *Railway World* and various other periodicals which appear at longer intervals, while the modeller is catered for by *Model Railways*, *Railway Modeller*, *Model Railway Constructor*, *Modelworld* and specialist journals covering engineering and plastic and international modelling. *Modern Railways* and *Railway Gazette International* are devoted to the current scene, *Modern Tramway* provides for the rapid transit and tramway enthusiast and publications like *European Railways Magazine* and *International Railway Journal* for those whose interests are in railways overseas. Radio London presents a regular railway programme called *Rail* on 94·9 VHF and 206 metres medium wave and other railway features are presented from time to time by Radio Blackburn, Radio Brighton, Radio Oxford, Radio Medway and Radio Leicester.

Finally, a few other addresses may be of use to the railway devotee:
Model Railway Club, Keen House, 4 Calshot Street, London N1
English Tourist Board, 4 Grosvenor Gardens, London SW1W 0DU
National Bus Company, 25 New Street Square, London EC4A 3AP
British Railways Board, 222 Marylebone Road, London NW1 6JJ
Department of the Environment, 2 Marsham Street, London SW1P 3EB

Reading List

Railway & Steam Enthusiasts' Handbook (Avon-Anglia)

Light Railway Handbook (Oakwood Press)

BR Pre-Grouping Atlas (Ian Allan)

Locomotion by O. S. Nock (Routledge & Kegan Paul)

History of Inland Transport & Communication by E. A. Pratt (David & Charles)

British Railway Signalling by Kichenside & Williams (Ian Allan)

Red For Danger by L. T. C. Rolt (David & Charles)

Regional Histories of the Railways of Great Britain (series) – David & Charles

Steam Horse: Iron Road (BBC)

Railway History Sources (Avon-Anglia)

Acknowledgements

Cover: No 1 *Taylyllyn* enters Rhydyronen station on the Talyllyn Railway with a train from Towyn. Copyright Allan Stewart. *General*: Geoffrey Body; Talyllyn Railway/J. F. Rimmer; Keighley & Worth Valley Light Railway; Romney, Hythe & Dymchurch Light Railway; J. B. Snell; London Transport; Quarry Tours Ltd; Scottish Railway Preservation Society; The Lord O'Neill; Dean Forest Railway Society; B. C. Baker; Great Western Railway Mus, Swindon; G. Wildish; S. C. Nash; BR Western Region; Dart Valley Railway; Brian Fisher; BR London Midland Region; BR Scottish Region; Michael Farr; Pritchard Patent Product Co; Pendon Museum

Index

David & Charles have a book on it

Railway Heraldry by George Dow. No product of the
Industrial Age was more colourful than the British steam-hauled
passenger train, but although colours might be shared one aspect of
railway decor always differed: the armorial devices. These
appeared on locomotives, stock, station buildings, uniforms and
correspondence, and this is the only reliable work of reference
(colour and black and white) on them. Illustrated. Also available
in paperback.

150 Years of British Steam Locomotives by Brian Reed.
Published to honour the 150th anniversary of the opening of the
Stockton & Darlington Railway, this book is a labour of love.
Profusely illustrated with blueprints and photographs – including
material not previously available – this is a unique pictorial history
of the locomotive in the British age of steam. Illustrated.

Steam Entertainment by John R. Hume & Baron F. Duckham.
A natural companion for *Railways for Pleasure* on your shelves. This
rounds out the picture: although the steam locomotive takes pride
of place, the book also covers steam tugs, launches, yachts,
fairground and traction engines. Living nostalgia for the
enthusiast. Illustrated. Also available in paperback.

The Great Way West by David St John Thomas. A tribute in
words and pictures to the unique 'Great Western' route, which
probably has a more fascinating history and passes through more
varied scenery than any other British railway of comparable
length. A book for all who love the Great Western, or who just
want to get more pleasure from their next train journey from
Paddington. Illustrated.

Steam, edited by Geoffrey Kichenside, a collection of pictures not to be missed, showing the publishers' love of the medium, the art of steam in action. It includes many photographs of the most famous trains and locomotives illustrated.

Steam in the West Riding by J. S. Whiteley and G. W. Morrison, the first of many David & Charles illustrated regional histories; a unique work of its kind.

A Regional History of the Railways of Great Britain — jointly edited history. Eight volumes, covering the South West, Eastern England, Greater London, North East England, Scotland, Ireland, the West Midlands, and Southern England; a work to delight the every railway enthusiast; photographs and ample reference. Illustrated.

The Great Little Railways of Wales by L. D. S. A collection of the narrow gauge railways of Wales; an appeal to those associated and important to the Welsh economy, in earlier days, the narrow gauge railways; what remains of such as operates today; incorporates many photographs; a superbly produced book — many of the photographs never published for the purpose.